WHAT IS
SPIRITUAL
ABOUT BEING
PUNCTUAL?

Ramesh Bijlani is a medical doctor, writer, teacher, scientist and above all, a person committed to using his unique blend of talents for touching the hearts and lives of his fellow beings. Educated at the All India Institute of Medical Sciences (AIIMS), New Delhi, and the Massachusetts Institute of Technology (MIT), Cambridge MA, the USA, Dr Bijlani spent nearly 30 years on the faculty of AIIMS. In 1992, he started going into the depths of yoga, especially the integral yoga of Sri Aurobindo and The Mother. In the year 2005, he took voluntary retirement from AIIMS to find more time for putting his blessings as a communicator to better use. Professor Bijlani was conferred an honorary doctorate in yoga by Swami Vivekananda Yoga Anusandhana Samsthana (S-VYASA), Bangalore, in 2006. Besides his research publications, popular articles and blogs, he has been the author of more than 25 published books. He stays and works at Sri Aurobindo Ashram, Delhi branch, where he gives inspirational talks, conducts spiritual retreats, mind-body workshops and yoga courses, and also continues to write.

WHAT IS
SPIRITUAL
ABOUT BEING
PUNCTUAL?

RAMESH BIJLANI

First published by
Rupa Publications India Pvt. Ltd 2022
7/16, Ansari Road, Daryaganj
New Delhi 110002

Sales Centres:
Allahabad Bengaluru Chennai
Hyderabad Jaipur Kathmandu
Kolkata Mumbai

Copyright © Ramesh Bijlani 2022
An earlier version was first published by Sri Aurobindo Ashram,
Delhi Branch, in 2018.

The views and opinions expressed in this book are the author's own and the facts are as reported by him which have been verified to the extent possible, and the publishers are not in any way liable for the same.

All rights reserved.
No part of this publication may be reproduced, transmitted,
or stored in a retrieval system, in any form or by any means,
electronic, mechanical, photocopying, recording or otherwise,
without the prior permission of the publisher.

ISBN: 978-93-5520-780-7

First impression 2022

10 9 8 7 6 5 4 3 2 1

The moral right of the author has been asserted.

Printed in India

This book is sold subject to the condition that it shall not,
by way of trade or otherwise, be lent, resold, hired out, or otherwise
circulated, without the publisher's prior consent, in any form of binding
or cover other than that in which it is published.

To
my spiritual masters

Sri Aurobindo
who revealed to me
the path

The Mother
who holds my hand
along the path

CONTENTS

Preface ix
Introduction xiii

1. Abstinence 1
2. Activism 7
3. Administration 15
4. Adoption 20
5. Advertising 24
6. Apologizing 27
7. Army 32
8. Business 36
9. Celebrations 41
10. Conferences 44
11. Conversation 49
12. DINK 53
13. Divorce 58
14. Driving 67
15. Entertainment 76
16. Forgiveness 79
17. Gambling 83
18. Gossip 86
19. Grihastha 92
20. Grumbling 99

21. Healthy Living	101
22. Internet	104
23. Leadership	111
24. Management	115
25. Marriage	121
26. Money	129
27. Parenting	134
28. Photography	141
29. Politics	147
30. Punctuality	153
31. Queue	155
32. Relationships	158
33. Sex Work	167
34. Shopping	171
35. Touch	176
36. War	181

PREFACE

If one wants to lead the spiritual life, one must not be three-fourths asleep.

—The Mother
(*The Great Adventure: A Diary for All Times*, p. 71)

According to Sri Aurobindo, every culture has a mental ideal, which expresses itself in its art, music, architecture, dance, etc., and also in the life and behaviour of its people. The mental ideal of the Indian culture is spirituality, and its imprint on India's creative arts is too obvious to be missed. Spirituality, at one time, also permeated every aspect of Indian life, and influenced how a person would eat, raise his children, conduct his business or resolve conflicts. Being spiritual did not hinder material progress; in fact, till about a thousand years ago, India was second to none in science and technology. Thus, India has a rich and vibrant culture in which a life-affirming brand of spirituality had a strong, all-pervasive presence. But somewhere along the way, there developed a dichotomy between spirituality and worldly life. Spirituality came to be seen as a sacred pursuit for a select few who renounced worldly life to pursue their passion for the deeper truths of existence in a cave or in the Himalayas. For the rest of the people, it was worldly life to which they professed to reconcile because they had been condemned to it by circumstances, but which they also secretly enjoyed. For them, spirituality got reduced to a few religious rituals which had lost its meaning, but to which they submitted either in the hope of material benefits or in an attempt to escape punishment for their misdeeds. This dichotomy has not really disappeared, and therefore it is easy to relate to even today. This dichotomy led to the degeneration of worldly life for which the country has paid, and continues to pay, a heavy price.

Sri Aurobindo made a powerful case for the life-affirming brand of spirituality. He was not alone in doing so. In fact, India had the good fortune of having, from the end of the nineteenth century onwards, many deeply spiritual leaders who observed how disappearance of spirituality from daily life had led to the decay of a flourishing culture—an eastern culture which could also be a model for today's materially saturated but spiritually starved countries of the West. Swami Vivekananda, Mahatma Gandhi, Rabindranath Tagore, and many others, each in his own way, tried to bring spirituality back into worldly life, not in an attempt to take the world back to the past but to bring the ancient Indian ideal back to enrich and ennoble today's world. In his literary works, Sri Aurobindo has touched just about every subject under the sun—history, science, education, psychology, sociology, medicine and what not—and has given every subject that he touched upon a unique and timeless spiritual orientation. The ashram that he and The Mother established at Pondicherry (now Puducherry) in 1926 was an experiment to see how far the ideal of doing worldly work with a spiritual attitude could be put into practice; the experiment was extended to the Delhi branch of the ashram when it was established in 1956. Another large-scale experiment was launched by The Mother in 1968 in the form of an international township, Auroville, near Puducherry. The overall success of all these experiments has shown that the modern world is not only compatible with but also undergoes a remarkable improvement when worldly activity is imbued with spirituality. The fact that the dichotomy between worldly life and spiritual life continues to dominate the Indian psyche is because deeply ingrained attitudes are difficult to change. The difficulty is not an excuse for inactivity, but only an explanation for the slow progress that is only to be expected.

Inspired by the work and mission of Sri Aurobindo and The Mother, this book presents more than 30 essays on topics that seem far removed from spirituality. These essays, dealing with mundane topics from a spiritual angle, demonstrate how nothing truly is beyond the scope of a spiritual approach to life. If punctuality can be a spiritual value, and advertising and driving can be spiritualized, there is nothing in life that cannot improve with the spiritual touch. If these essays can be of any help at all to India, which has just started recovering from the degeneration initiated by the dichotomy between spirituality and worldly life, the effort will be worthwhile. And, as Sri Aurobindo said in his famous Uttarpara speech: when India rises, it rises not for itself but for the world.

New Delhi
27 December 2017

INTRODUCTION

Whose Spirit Is Spirituality About?

To be vigilant is not merely to resist what pulls you downward, but above all to be alert in order not to lose any opportunity to progress, any opportunity to overcome a weakness, to resist a temptation, any opportunity to learn something, to correct something, to master something.

—The Mother
(*The Great Adventure: A Diary for All Times*, p. 72)

Spirituality is one way to answer basic existential questions, such as the origin of the material universe; the relationship between the Creator of the universe, if there was one, and Its creation; and the role and place of the individual in the plan that the Creator might have for Its creation. The answers that spirituality provides to these questions have endured the longest and have bounced back after every attempt to wipe them out. The answers that spirituality provides are: first, the material universe is not an accident; it was consciously created by the

Creator. It is a powerful being that knows everything and can do everything. Secondly, the Spirit of this all-knowing, all-powerful being has an all-pervasive presence in Its creation. And finally, the Creator continues to play a role in running the universe. On these three basic tenets, there is total agreement between the spiritual philosophies underlying all religions.

Thus, the word spirituality has been derived from 'spirit', which here, is the Spirit of the Creator. The Spirit of the Creator is present in every bit of the creation. It is called the Spirit because it is always present; it is fundamental to the very existence of the creation, and yet, it is not very obvious. For example, when we say that the spirit of the painter is there in her painting, what we mean is that although what we see easily is only a landscape or a portrait, some unique element of the personality of the painter has also entered the painting. Similarly, the Creator also has an invisible presence throughout Its creation. It is this invisible presence that is called the Spirit.

Vedanta, the best known spiritual philosophy of the Hindu tradition, goes one step further. It does not look upon the Creator and Its creation as two separate entities. It says that the Creator did not create the creation; It became the creation. Thus, the creation is nothing but the Creator itself in another form. This makes the all-pervasive presence of the Creator in the creation a natural corollary. For example, suppose a child takes a square piece of paper, folds it and makes a boat out of it. Now the paper has become the boat. The boat is nothing but the paper in another form. No arguments are necessary to prove that the boat contains the paper—it is paper! Similarly, no arguments are required to prove that the creation contains the Creator—it is the Creator. The Creator is One; hence the expression, One in all. The One has been called by many names. In this book, It will generally be called the Divine; sometimes, It will be called God, the Infinite or Consciousness (with a capital C); occasionally, It may be called by some other names.

Is spirituality only a philosophy?

Philosophy is based on rational analysis. But no amount of rational analysis can prove spiritual truths. The confidence in asserting spiritual truths comes not from rational analysis but from the fact that some rare individuals have actually 'seen' these truths; they have experienced them. These are the people called rishis (*ri*: to see) in the Hindu tradition. In the Judaic and Christian traditions, they are called mystics; in the Islamic tradition, they are called Sufis. The interesting thing is that the independently arrived at experiences of the rishis, Sufis and mystics have been remarkably similar in spite of being separated by time and tradition. Comparable descriptions of mystic experience from different traditions have been brought together in one place by Aldous Huxley in his book *The Perennial Philosophy* (Harper & Brothers, 1945). Thus, spiritual truths are not philosophy; they are the result of experience which only those who have resorted to intense concentration of effort and extreme self-purification have received. Experience is always at a much higher level than philosophy or mental knowledge. Suppose a person has never eaten any sweet. If we tell him that sweetness is a very pleasant taste, it is the result of adding sugar to a food, such foods are called sweets, and we also give him a few recipes for making sweets, he will still not know what sweetness is. On the other hand, if we give him a sweet and tell him to put it in his mouth, he at once knows what sweetness is, because now he has experienced it. If that is true of a simple sensory experience like sweetness, how much more true it is of the mystical experience, which comes not from the senses but from 'divine eyes' (*divyachakshu*, the Gita 11:8)—which only the chosen ones get from the Divine. While spirituality is based on experience, spiritual truths can be rationalized. Rationalized spiritual truths are spiritual philosophy. That is why in Sanskrit, philosophy is called *darshan* (seeing). A totally mind-boggling rationalization of spiritual truths has been provided by Sri Aurobindo in his classic, *The Life Divine*.

Is spirituality only an academic discipline?

Spirituality is not just something to learn for the sake of knowing more, and certainly it is not mere intellectual entertainment. It has important practical implications. It gives us a fundamental basis for the oneness of creation. Since we are all born of the same source and have the Spirit of the same Divine pervading us, we are all inter-related. And, it is easy to understand how a sense of oneness can improve the quality of life in the world. However, knowing spirituality at a theoretical level is not enough to organize our life around it. All life can be organized around spiritual truths only by being constantly aware of them or being conscious of them. Being constantly aware of spiritual truths and not being aware of them at all are two poles of consciousness.

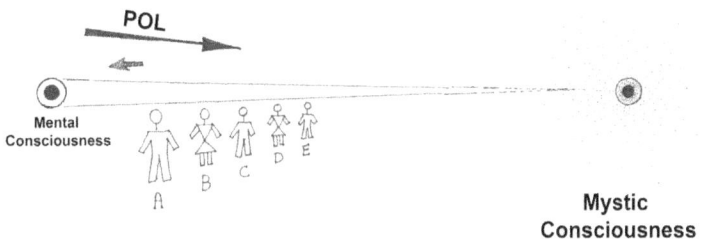

The two poles of consciousness. The purpose of life (PoL) is to take a few steps towards the mystic consciousness. A-E, individuals at different points on the spectrum between the two poles.

At *one pole* of consciousness, we are not at all aware of the deeper layer of reality revealed by spirituality. Our picture of reality at this pole is based on sensory experience, past experience and logic. This pole may be called the *mental consciousness*. At the *other pole* is the consciousness which is aware of whatever is known at the level of the mental consciousness, but it is also aware of a deeper layer of reality that resides within, behind and beyond the reality based on the mental consciousness. This wider, deeper and higher consciousness is the *mystic consciousness*. Between these two poles is a whole wide spectrum, and the consciousness of the majority of mankind is somewhere on that spectrum. But the important point is that the point on this spectrum where we are today need not be the point where we stay all our lives. We can take a few steps in either direction during our lifetime. And, taking a few steps towards the mystic consciousness is the true purpose of human life. This is a process that is called the growth of consciousness or spiritual growth. It is called growth of consciousness because, through this process, consciousness is growing higher, deeper and wider. It is also called spiritual growth because, through this process, the person grows in a direction that makes her more aware of the all-pervasive Spirit of the Divine.

The question that you may ask is why you should adopt a purpose of life defined by somebody else. The answer to that question is that adopting this purpose of life is the only way to get true happiness, and happiness is something we all want. This rather cryptic and dogmatic statement will become easier to understand by the end of this chapter. But at this stage, one might just say that fulfilling this purpose of life depends on becoming a good person and progressing from being good to becoming a better person. Becoming a good person leads to happiness; becoming a better person leads to still more happiness. An interesting question was raised by Victor Hugo in his novel, *Les Miserables*: 'Are we happy because we are good; or are we good because we are happy?' Victor Hugo's verdict and the time-tested verdict is unanimous: we are happy because we are good.

How can the purpose of life be addressed?

There are three principal ways in which the purpose of life may be addressed: making the right moral choices; adopting an enlightened attitude to work; and looking upon the vicissitudes of life as opportunities.

Making choices

Life is a series of choices, many of which have moral implications. Further, as we proceed on the spiritual path, more and more choices acquire moral implications. In any journey, choices made at crossroads and T-junctions determine whether we go towards or away from the goal. The moral choices that we make have the same crucial importance in the journey of life. For making these choices, we have two obvious and noisy tools, and also a hidden and non-assertive tool. One obvious and extremely powerful tool is the emotional part of the being, which pulls us towards what feels good. The other obvious, and rather malleable, tool is our intellect, which tries, often unsuccessfully, to guide us towards choices that are the most profitable in material terms in the long run and, at the same time, least risky. Intellect uses reason, but reason is a versatile instrument. It can justify just about anything. That is why the intellect is amenable to exploitation by feelings; the heart can drive the head. The hidden tool is our divine essence, often called the soul. The soul is there not just to console us with the idea that we are essentially immortal, and because our soul is immortal, it also has a dynamic aspect, which participates in daily life and provides us with the best moral choices. Sri Aurobindo calls this dynamic aspect of the soul 'our psychic being'. To understand this tool, let us take an example from a film dialogue.

The film is *Saath Saath*, starring Farooq Sheikh and Deepti Naval. The hero starts off as an idealistic young boy, and the heroine likes him for that. Then, the hero and heroine get married and have a baby. Now, the hero starts feeling that unless they have more money, the family will never have a physically comfortable life. To make more money, he starts getting corrupt. Finally, one day, he brings a powerful person home, serves him dinner, and at the end of the meal, hands him an envelope containing some money. After the guest has gone, his wife takes him to task. She says, 'What has happened to you? I could not even imagine you could stoop to such low levels.' The hero replies, 'Look here, I haven't created this world; I just live in it. And, whatever is necessary for survival in this world, I do just that. And, after all, for whose sake am I doing all this? I am doing it for you and the baby.' What is happening here is that the hero *feels* like doing something. When questioned, he justifies it by giving some *reasons*. In other words, he lets his feelings exploit his intellect. His feelings now invent reasons to justify what he feels like doing at the emotional level. Further, when he says, 'I am doing it for you and the baby', he is trying to direct his wife's feelings to exploit her intellect in the same way. However, while he is feeling very clever, a voice from somewhere deep within tells him, 'You are wrong; she is right.' This voice is just a whisper, but it is recurrent and persistent; and although it does not go into any arguments, it is extremely clear. The emotional part of his being wants something, and his intellect has justified it. In other words, his feelings and his thoughts have reached some sort of an understanding. If that is so, where is this dissenting voice —the voice that just says, 'You are wrong; she is right'—coming from? This voice is obviously coming from neither the emotional nor the intellectual part of the being. It is coming from his divine essence, the psychic being. The voice of the psychic being is shy and faint, but it is quick and clear. Without going into any arguments, in an instant, it just gives its verdict about what is right and what is wrong. It leaves us in no doubt about what is the right thing to do. But since it is content to be ignored, while the feelings and the intellect are very noisy, the faint voice of the psychic being often gets ignored. However, it has a way of getting its way at least sometimes. That happens because we can anticipate that if we listen to the voice of the psychic being, we will get immense joy and lasting mental peace. We can also foresee that if we act contrary to the verdict of the psychic being, we will feel guilty and would get recurrent uneasiness. It is to get the reward of joy and lasting mental peace, and to escape the punishment of guilt and recurrent uneasiness that we do listen to this voice at least sometimes.

As you might have guessed, it is the choices based on the voice of the psychic being that take us towards the goal of life. These choices are not only morally the best, they also give us joy and lasting mental peace. But that is not all that they give us. They also play a role in transforming the emotional part of the being and the intellect. Transformation of the emotional part of the being means that now, it starts valuing the joy and lasting mental peace coming from the right choices, and starts advocating the same choices as the psychic being. Transformation of the intellect means that it now habitually gives us reasons that justify the choices of the psychic being. As a result of this twin transformation, conflict starts disappearing from life. Further, choices of the psychic being involve giving money, time, an object or giving up a temptation. Giving is in our own hands; getting is not. Therefore, the joy that arises from making the right choices is always in our own hands. That is why, it is said that the source of true happiness is within us. Discovering this source of happiness gives us control over our sense of well-being. Finally, making the best moral choices gives us a sense of satisfaction, which is best described as fulfilment, or a feeling of wanting nothing. Joy, lasting mental peace, reduction in conflict, control over our happiness and fulfilment—all these translate into good mental health. And, modern medicine has rediscovered that good mental health also promotes good physical health. Good physical and mental health is what everyone wants, and very few get because the rest keep looking for what they want in the wrong places. If making certain choices gives us everything we want, and also fulfils the purpose of life, one cannot ask for a better combination.

Attitude towards work

Grumbling about the type of work we have been condemned to do, getting upset over the unintended outcomes of our work, complaining about not getting enough appreciation for the work that we do are not only a major source of stress in the world, they are also very unspiritual attitudes. The spiritual attitude to work is to treat the work that we have to do as an opportunity to serve the Divine, and to offer the work to the Divine who has given us the unique talents, abilities and opportunities that make the work possible. We should do the work to the best of our abilities so that it is fit to be offered to the Divine, and yet, we should accept whatever the outcome of the work is as an expression of the Divine Will and Wisdom. This attitude not only takes away the usual work-related stress, it also makes work our vehicle for going towards the goal of our life. The attitude applies not only to professional work or the work that we do for a living; it applies just as much to household work and parenting. Again, one cannot ask for a better combination. Of course, it is understood that in the moral choices that we have to make in the course of doing our work, we should let the voice of the psychic being prevail.

Vicissitudes of life as opportunities

Even making the best moral choices and having a spiritual attitude to work does not make us immune to the ups and downs of life. What is viewed as pleasant and what is perceived as unpleasant are both opportunities for fulfilling the purpose of life. Misfortunes and traumatic events are an opportunity to make us conscious of our limitations, make us humble and helpful while dealing with our fellow beings, and make us turn to the One who has no limitations. Good fortunes, such as success and wealth, are an opportunity to be grateful to the Divine without whose unseen hand such experiences would not have come to us, and to share the fruits of our fortune with those of our fellow beings who can benefit from it. In practice, misfortune acts as a more frequent trigger for moving towards the goal of life than good fortune. These attitudes to good fortune and misfortune not only help us achieve equanimity, they also contribute to fulfilling the purpose of life. Again, one cannot ask for a better combination.

How much of life can spirituality occupy?

If spirituality can enter the choices that we make, the ups and downs of our life, and also the very work that we do, what else is left? Obviously, spirituality can occupy all life, or to put it in one of Sri Aurobindo's most celebrated quotes, 'All life is yoga', which means that all life gives us an opportunity for the practice of yoga, or all life is suitable as a field for the practice of yoga. Why should anyone fill their life with spirituality? The answer to that question is obvious from the above discussion. We should let our life be permeated with spirituality not just because it fulfils the purpose of life, as defined by somebody else, but because it gives just about everything everybody is looking for. What follows are 30 essays showing how so many things that we do not habitually associate with spirituality could actually be an opportunity for fulfilling the purpose of life, and getting as by-products everything that we are looking for.

ABSTINENCE

Plugging the Big Leak

All the things I really like to do are immoral, illegal or fattening.

—Alexander Woollcott

There is a widespread belief in India that a man on the spiritual path should keep away from sexual activity because sexual activity leads to ejaculation, and ejaculation of semen drains energy. Correspondingly, great pride is associated with the number of years for which a man has been able to successfully retain his semen. This raises at least three questions. Is it true? If it is true, why and how? And, if it is true, are women fortunate in being exempt from this restraint?

Is it true?

Yes, there is a grain of truth in the belief.

If it is true, why and how?

Sex is a major preoccupation of man. The way we are constituted, the preoccupation is natural. It is a preoccupation that runs through the animal kingdom. If an animal does not have a mate during the mating season, it is miserable. It can also anticipate that if it finds a mate, it will be happy. Escaping misery and getting the anticipated joy is what motivates the animal to go to great lengths to find a mate. By coupling sex with strong emotions, nature has ensured survival of the species. Man is also an animal, and therefore, a similar preoccupation is not surprising. But man is also much more than a feeding and breeding animal. Probably why, in man, there is no season dedicated entirely to mating. Man should be doing what is uniquely human, for example, accumulating knowledge, acquiring wisdom, generating knowledge, creating art and literature, and, above all, working towards growth of consciousness. Even if we forget about all these activities, man is also unique in having babies who are born totally helpless and therefore need prolonged care, which can best be given by both parents together. The human male is, therefore, not exempt from childcare, unlike in many animals where the male is free to roam, impregnating one female after another. Since everything important and worthwhile drains a lot of energy, man, to truly be man, can afford to indulge in sex only to the extent vital for the essential function of limited and regulated procreation. In short, it is a question of priorities. For man, sex is, or at least should be, low down on the list of priorities. For a man on the spiritual path, sex disappears from the list altogether. It disappears because what the spiritual seeker pursues needs all his energy and attention, leaving no room for a dispensable activity such as sex.

Sex is no doubt a source of joy even to man, but man is also capable of moving on from sex to other higher, more dependable and more enduring sources of happiness. Overcoming attachment to the lower by replacing it with an attachment to something higher is the process by which man achieves personal growth. The final rung of the process is to *replace attachment* to all worldly activities, possessions and relationships with the attachment to the Divine; worldly activities may continue, necessary possessions may continue to be held, and love and kindness in relationships may also continue, *but without the attachment.* Thus, spiritual life is not dull or joyless. It is a life in which the joy of being with the Eternal replaces the attachment to pleasures that come from what does not and cannot last.

Are women fortunate in being exempt from this restraint?

Yes, in a way they are, but to say that it is because women cannot have an ejaculation would be rather too simplistic and superficial. In women, restraint needs less effort than in men because of a basic gender difference. Women are, in general, far less preoccupied with sex than men. For women, the primary need is love. To get that love, they also indulge in sex. In contrast, men often love women because that helps them have sex. That is why, a man can have sex with his wife even after a bitter quarrel during the day, but his wife may be unwilling. 'How can I have sex with a man who has been so nasty to me during the day,' says she. If she rejects him at night, the next day the man might be even more nasty. 'How can I be nice to a woman who does not even let me have sex,' says he. Since the primary need of women is love, they move on rather easily from love for a man to love for their children. From there, those who have an aspiration for a spiritual life easily move on to love for the Divine. In short, developing a detachment from sex is for spiritual life—a necessity in both men and women. For women, this task is easier because their urge is weaker, not because they cannot have an ejaculation.

Closing thoughts

Spiritual quest is an inner change which gets reflected in outer life. The inner change is about moving away from the lower to the higher, from the fleeting to the Eternal, from the fragile to the Imperishable. Moving towards the Eternal and Imperishable, also called Brahman, is what Brahmacharya literally means. The movement leads to an 'easy and natural' detachment from many things that were earlier very important, interesting or pleasurable. Detachment from sex is only one aspect of this general process. Thus, Brahmacharya is not really celibacy; it is overcoming one's attachment to sensory pleasures, sex being one of them. As the attachment disappears, the activity itself might disappear if it is not indispensable.

Thus, attachment to food might disappear, but eating still goes on. But when attachment to sex disappears, sex itself disappears from life. Retention of semen is only an outer symbol of the disappearance of the sexual urge and sexual activity. This outer symbol obviously cannot apply to women, but the process is essentially the same irrespective of gender.

Presence of the Divine in the creation is all-pervasive; the same Divine manifests as matter and as man. The Divine is all-knowing and all-powerful. Hence there is Infinite Intelligence encapsulated in each atom of man. Human life is essentially about discovering, tapping and channeling this Infinite Intelligence. This Infinite source may languish largely undiscovered; a small fraction of it may be dissipated unconsciously as useless thoughts and fruitless actions, or even worse, as negative thoughts and destructive actions—which is the worst form of brain drain; it may also be dissipated through sexual activity. Conserving the limited fraction of the Infinite Intelligence at our command for better things not only makes us more productive, it also helps in tapping a bigger fraction; in other words, we can then manifest more of our potential. Spiritual quest takes this process of conservation and optimal channeling to its logical conclusion. That is why it aims at conserving the maximum of which retention of semen is a tangible outcome. The other tangible outcomes may be sublime art and poetry, tales of miraculous healing, as well as tremendous feats of endurance. But these impressive results, although possible, are not what spirituality is about or for. It is about the Divine, and for the Divine; all else is incidental. What is incidental is dross; the gold is only the Divine.

> *If the sexual impulse comes, do not be sorry or troubled but look at it calmly, quiet it down, reject all wrong suggestions connected with it and wait for the Higher Consciousness to transform it into the true force and Ananda.*
>
> Sri Aurobindo

∞

First published as a blog on 27 December 2016
Link: https://www.speakingtree.in/blog/plugging-the-leak

ACTIVISM

Whence and Whither Activism?

The rolling cycles passed and came again,
Brought the same toils and the same barren end,
Forms ever new and ever old, the long
Appalling revolutions of the world.

—Sri Aurobindo (*Savitri*, Book 10, Canto 4, p. 643)

An activist is an angry person. She is angry not because of a personal insult but because her sense of what the world should be like has been insulted by the way the world actually is. She is generally right and the world wrong. That is why her anger is called righteous anger. And there is so much wrong with the world that it is not difficult for a sensitive person to find an issue worth her wrath. Her wrath unleashes a tremendous amount of energy. Her enthusiasm is infectious and she is able to inspire many more to join hands with her. The result is a movement, a crusade. The intention is to change the world a wee bit by eliminating at least one evil—be it child labour, gender inequality, poverty, corruption or environmental degradation.

What does activism achieve?

The outcome of activism is generally disappointing. And, this is not because an activist picks up only one issue while there are so many issues begging for attention. One group of activists may address only one issue, but all such groups put together end up addressing almost all the ills afflicting society. History shows that all the activists put together have, in the long run, achieved precious little. Activists, social workers and reformers have come and gone, but the problems have persisted. If some problems have eased somewhat, they have been replaced by a new set of problems. Not only that, even the problems that seemed to be over have returned with a vengeance after a lull. The world has continued to be a place full of inequality and injustice, and the consequent misery and suffering—a place characterized by *dukkha* (sorrow), as Lord Buddha declared more than 2,500 years ago.

Why the failure?

The failure of all the activists of all times has not been due to lack of vigour, vitality or sincerity, or the willingness to struggle or sacrifice, or the seriousness of purpose. Activists have given generously, suffered happily, fought courageously and persevered patiently in pursuit of their aims. The failure has been because of one basic flaw: all movements and revolutions have addressed the symptoms, not the root cause. The root cause of each one of the issues picked up by activists is the average level of human consciousness. Human consciousness is, or rather so far has been, primarily and typically, an ego-driven consciousness. Ego concentrates the person's attention on himself. For the individual, his needs and aspirations acquire top priority. To him, his cold is more important than somebody else's cancer. So long as this type of consciousness continues to be the norm, the powerful will continue to oppress the weak, the rich will continue to exploit the poor and the mighty will continue to terrify the meek. In simple words, unless human nature changes significantly for the better, the problems of human existence will continue, as they have for thousands of years.

Is it futile?

If all previous efforts to solve the problems of human existence have failed, does it mean that activism is simply activity without achievement? No, it is still worthwhile for at least three reasons. First, it may not be a lasting solution for the problems, but it does mitigate the problems, makes them manageable and prevents them from growing bigger. It at least makes those affected by the problems feel that somebody cares. Second, it provides the activists an opportunity for spiritual growth, which is the very purpose of life. Spiritual growth occurs through genuine acts of love. Genuine acts of love require the one who loves to give something that the one who is being loved needs. Activism provides that fit. The activist has the time, energy and some of the qualities and resources that are required to address the issue. Those affected by the issue need this type of help. Thus, by giving what she has to those who need it, the activist is able to grow spiritually. But the degree of growth would depend on the attitude, the intention and the motive behind the action. Maximum growth would occur if the activist has the attitude of being an instrument of the Divine, is totally selfless and is motivated by true love. This attitude not only leads to maximum spiritual growth, it also is the best defence against frustration. If the activist starts evaluating the result of her activity in terms of measurable outcomes such as the extent to which the issue addressed by her has disappeared, sooner or later she is likely to be frustrated. What she has to remember is that she is not helping anybody. Those whom she thinks she is trying to help are actually helping her by giving her an opportunity for spiritual growth. If she uses the opportunity well through the right attitude to her work, her spiritual growth is the one outcome that is guaranteed, one hundred per cent. But this is an outcome that is not measurable. Finally, spiritual growth of the activist is a contribution to the rise in the consciousness of the human race, which is the next major step in the evolution of life on the planet. But this outcome also cannot be measured, at least not easily or reliably. In short, activism and its close cousins, such as social work or charity, are not futile although it may seem so if their outcome is evaluated by their measurable impact on the problems addressed. That is why The Mother has said that 'the mind is incapable of judging spiritual things'.

When will the problems be solved?

That the earth has been a place full of suffering for thousands of years does not mean that it is destined to be so forever. The root cause of suffering is human nature, which in turn depends on the level of human consciousness. Although human consciousness has a wide spectrum, the quality of life on earth depends on the average human consciousness. The beauty of the human consciousness, however, is that it can rise as a result of spiritual growth. Further, an urge for spiritual growth has been planted in us by the Divine. If more and more people on earth consciously live in such a way as to grow spiritually, the average level of consciousness would eventually rise. Sri Aurobindo and The Mother have given us the assurance that such a movement is round the corner. There are several signs that this is neither wishful thinking, nor a utopian dream. First, what Sri Aurobindo and The Mother said about a hundred years ago, is today being said by so many spiritual thinkers. Here is a sample of quotes from some of them.

'We are evolving from five-sensory humans into multi-sensory humans.'[1]

'The collective level of consciousness of mankind remained at 190 for many centuries and, curiously, only jumped to its current level of 204 within the last decade.'[2]

---

[1] Zukav, Gary, *The Seat of the Soul*, Simon & Schuster, New York, 1989, pp. 13-21.
[2] Hawkins, David, *Power versus Force: An Anatomy of Consciousness: The Hidden Determinants of Human Behaviour,* Veritas Publishing, Arizona, 1998, p. 67.

'Today, across the world, people are awakening as if from a deep sleep. There is a powerful desire to heal and be healed. ... The passion for healing is leading to a transformation of individual and collective consciousness.'[3]

'What we are experiencing is a generational transition from dominantly material modes of existence to emerging life and consciousness modes.'[4]

Second, there is a movement away from religions towards spirituality; not the spirituality based on scriptures and life-negation, but that based on the inner Light and life-affirmation. Third, there is an increasing convergence of spirituality and secular knowledge embodied in disciplines such as physics, psychology, neurophysiology and medicine. Fourth, more and more young people are moving away from industry, banking and business towards non-greed-driven vocations for making a living: activism is one of them. Finally, the internet is compelling unprecedented transparency in public life, making it difficult for governments and businesses to cheat, stupefy or befool people. Facts and figures also point in the same direction. Deaths in genocides and other mass killings, number of armed conflicts and wars, and deaths in armed conflicts have all shown a declining trend in the last two decades.[5] Based on comprehensive global surveys,

---

[3]de Carteret, Nikki, *Soul Power: The Transformation That Happens When You Know*, O Books, Hants, UK, 2003, p. 100, p. 282.
[4]Partho, 'The Emerging Consciousness Paradigm', *The Awakening Ray*, vol. 20, no. 1, 29 February 2016, pp. 21-23.
[5]Pinker, Steven and Andrew Mack, 'The World Is Not Falling Apart', *Reader's Digest,* India, January 2016, p. 74.

it has been 'concluded that a new global culture and consciousness have taken root and are beginning to grow in the world.'[6] These are all signs of an emerging new world order, an order that will be based on an unprecedented sense of oneness among human beings.

In short, we can look forward to a significant rise in the average level of human consciousness in the very near future. This rise will change human nature, or tilt the balance in favour of the best that is in man. When the affairs of the world will be conducted from the new plane of consciousness, we can hope for a final solution to the problems of human existence.

Conclusion

Activism that originates in an inner urge to give what we have to someone who needs it helps the activist grow spiritually, and thereby taking a few steps towards the fulfilment of the purpose of her life. Each individual who grows spiritually also makes a contribution towards raising the average consciousness of the human race. It is a perceptibly higher average human consciousness that will eventually solve the problems of evil and injustice, and the consequent misery and suffering that have characterized life on earth since time immemorial. Thus, activists are changing the world by contributing to the collective rise

---

[6]Elgin, Duane and Coleen LeDrew, 'Global Consciousness Change: Indicators of an Emerging Paradigm', *The Awakening Ray*, vol. 20, no. 1, 29 February 2016, pp. 15-16.

in consciousness. The specific problem that each activist is addressing may not be solved as quickly as we may like, but by doing what the activist is doing, she is taking a small step towards solving all the problems of human existence. If more and more of us organize our lives consciously around our highest level of consciousness, not only would we individually experience lasting mental peace and fulfilment, we would also be accelerating the process whereby life on the planet would undergo a lasting transformation. To contribute to the process, all of us do not have to turn to activism. But all of us have something to give, and there is someone in the world who needs what we can give. All we have to do is to discover what we are best equipped to give in view of our unique talents, gifts, temperament and circumstances, and give it to those who need it. Some of us may have knowledge, some money, some time and some may have only a smile to give. If we resolve to give it, the Divine will create the circumstances in which we can fulfil ourselves and manifest the divinity in us through self-giving. That is the Divine's way of slowly but surely working out Its design for the world.

∞

First published as a blog on 12 September 2016
Link: https://www.speakingtree.in/blog/whence-and-whither-activism

ADMINISTRATION

Papers, Problems and People

The sublimity of administration consists in knowing the proper degree of power that should be exerted on different occasions.

—Charles de Montesquieu

Administration has many levels, right from the lowly clerical jobs to the top management jobs in multinational corporations. The higher levels of administration are these days called management, and what transcends management is leadership. At the cost of oversimplification, one might say that a clerk deals with papers, a manager is concerned about fixing problems, and a leader knows that it is ultimately the people who matter the most. Irrespective of these differences, all administration is essentially about getting work done and keeping things moving. There is a general feeling that for work to be done and for things to keep moving, what one needs is tact, firmness, subtlety, and quite a bit of cunning, chicanery, manoeuvering, jugglery and that very

Indian device called jugaad.[1] Where, then, is the place for spirituality in this very down-to-earth activity?

Papers

Hidden behind the papers that land at an administrator's desk are people wanting permissions, a benefit, an exemption, etc. At a rational level, the decision should depend on the rules applicable. Assuming that the relevant rules do exist, there are still many fuzzy areas. How does the administrator interpret the rules? Are the rules applied impartially in all similar cases? Does the interpretation of rules depend exclusively on the merits of the present case, or is the official biased by the general impression he has about the person whose file he is looking at? If there is scope for the official's discretion, is that power used to help deserving cases or to punish somebody? Is the help doled out as a favour to someone known to me, related to me, referred to me by a friend, or to someone who has earlier done me a favour? Or is the help considered a privilege and an opportunity to make sure that rules do not become an excuse for injustice? And finally, if rules for dealing with the situation at hand do not exist, how

---

[1] Jugaad (alternatively *Juggaar*) is a colloquial Hindi and Punjabi word, which has various meanings depending on the situation. Roughly translated, jugaad is a 'hack'. It could also refer to an innovative fix or a simple work-around, a solution that bends the rules, or a resource that can be used in such a way. It is also often used to signify creativity— to make existing things work, or to create new things with meager resources.

does the administrator decide to say 'yes' or 'no' to what is being asked for? These are all questions that call for a choice. As in other situations in life, here also the choices can be made using three basic tools, which may or may not lead to the same choice. The three tools are feelings, rational analysis and the voice of the deepest Self. Feelings might guide us towards favouritism or revenge; reason might tell us to follow the rule book blindly because that is the safest thing to do; whereas the voice of the deepest Self, generally called the inner voice or the voice of the soul, guides us towards choices driven by universal and unconditional love. It is the last one that is the reference guide—the guide that never fails us, the guide that leads us towards spiritual growth. This growth comes from the love behind it, the love that is universal in the sense that it does not care for who the beneficiary is, and it is unconditional in that it does not depend on what that person has done or not done to me in the past.

Problems

The world is full of problems, and nobody can solve all of them. But there are individuals in positions that bring them in contact with a small sample of problems, and they are approached because it is often possible for them to take an action that can solve, or at least minimize, those problems. The person who can take action can behave in an egoistic fashion, take the action guided by his whims and fancies, and take his own sweet time to take the action. Or, he may derive sadistic pleasure by refusing to take action and spend his energies on finding reasons for doing nothing. All these attitudes exist in the world, but none is the spiritual attitude. The spiritual attitude for the person is to consider that his capacity to do something to ease the problem of a fellow human being is a privilege given to him by the Divine. The least he can do is to use his capacity to do what the Divine has given him this privilege for. Further, he should be grateful for the capacity that he has been given and the opportunity to use the capacity. Thus, he is not helping the person whose problem he is solving; that person is helping him by providing him an opportunity to use his capacity to help grow spiritually, and thereby fulfil the purpose of his life.

People

While the papers or the problems that an administrator has to deal with also have people behind them, the leader does not always wait for papers or problems to be presented to him. He thinks empathetically of the people whose life can be changed for the better by some of his actions or decisions. Then he takes the initiative to take those actions or decisions. He treats his position as good fortune that has been bestowed upon him by the Divine. He uses it to help his fellow beings, and thereby grows spiritually. But he looks at the situation only as an opportunity that the Divine has provided him through his fellow beings for fulfilling the purpose of his life.

Closing thoughts

During the Second World War, there was a Japanese diplomat, Chiune Sugihara, posted in Lithuania. One morning he woke up to the clamour of thousands of people who had assembled outside the embassy. He was told that they were Jews who had fled from Poland to escape death at the hands of Hitler and wanted visas for going to Japan. Giving thousands of visas at one go, and that too to refugees, was a serious issue, and therefore he consulted his government. Those were the days of telex messages. In the first message, the answer was 'no'; the second message, the answer was also 'no'; the third message, the answer, as expected, was still 'no'. His official duty was to follow the instructions of his government. But his inner voice told him to use his position to help these people escape death. He issued the visas and was called back to Japan, but he succeeded in saving the lives of thousands of people. He faced disciplinary action in Japan for it, but what he gained was beyond measure: the joy of giving, lasting mental peace and fulfilment.

∞

First published as a blog on 29 December 2016
Link: https://www.speakingtree.in/blog/papers-problems-and-people

ADOPTION

There Are No Others

... to feel love and oneness is to live.

—Sri Aurobindo (*Savitri*, Book 12, p. 724)

Infertility clinics are a big business. The business thrives on a widespread intense desire among couples who have failed to conceive in a reasonable time to somehow have a child of their own. When told something simple, something that they already know, that there are so many children waiting for adoption, the implied suggestion to adopt meets stiff resistance, which is generally justified by arguments that they would like to have a child with their genes, that they would like to leave behind in the world somebody who will carry their name, their legacy. None of these arguments are, in fact, a good reason for rejecting the option of adoption. What is the guarantee that our genes will produce a child better than the child we adopt; the adopted child might have a better combination of genes. Further, the adopted child is in front of us, whereas the child yet to come is a gamble; even 'normal' people can carry abnormal genes, which may show up in the child. Leaving a name behind in the world as a legacy is not the best practice; a much more important thing to worry about is raising a good human being. In fact, behind all the heroic and expensive efforts that the couple goes through in the infertility clinics is the desire not to just have a child but to have a child through whom the couple can extend its collective ego.

From the spiritual angle, all the conditions and circumstances we get in life are given to us as vehicles for fulfilling the purpose of life, which is spiritual growth. For some couples, infertility is also one of those conditions, and therefore a part of their vehicle. However, the vehicle is only an opportunity—to use it or to waste it is up to us. In general, the purpose of life is fulfilled best by giving what we have to those who need it. Here, the infertile couple has the desire to have a child, they have the capacity to take care of the child and there are children who need what the couple not only has but is very eager to give. To give it to a child who is not related to them by blood is a challenge life has thrown at them. If the challenge is met by treating the adopted child as their own, the spiritual growth will be more than if the child was actually their own. This happens because treating one's own child well is in keeping with the surface reality. But treating an adopted child in the same way is giving a practical expression to a deeper reality. The deeper reality is that we are all manifestations of the same Divine, or in simpler words, we are all children of the same God. When we give practical expression to a truth, we are on the way to realizing the truth. Realizing the oneness that characterizes all of us in spite of all the superficial differences is what spiritual growth is about. Hence, infertility is not a misfortune; it is a blessing in disguise. It is an uncommon opportunity given to selected people for accelerated spiritual growth.

Genes are only one of the determinants of what a human being turns out to be like. A lot depends on the upbringing and the environment. In terms of Vedanta, a lot also depends on the impressions carried by the individual from previous lives. Added to that is the way the individual uses the free will that all of us have been given by the Divine. The parents play a limited role in this complex process by contributing to the upbringing and the environment. They should try to do their best, but leave the outcome to the Divine. Parenthood is like writing. *A newborn is just the first draft, parenting edits it. Good editing can do wonders.* Couples that adopt a child have an opportunity to do that wonder; it doesn't really matter who wrote the first draft.

Adopting a child is an opportunity available to all, even to those who have children of their own. If a couple have a child of their own and still adopt a child, treating the two children alike is a still bigger challenge than that faced by the couple who do not have a biological child of their own. If the challenge is met, in terms of spiritual growth, it will be correspondingly more significant.

Strictly speaking, adoption does not necessarily mean adopting a child. Adoption just means accepting as one's own. Accepting as one's own requires breaking the ego barrier that divides us from others. The hammer that breaks the barrier is love. Family life provides good practice for loving, but love does not have to remain restricted to the family. Expanding the circle of love is a lifelong process. In fact, it has been seen that people who live long have one thing in common. They accept as their own anyone who is around them. They never fall short of objects of love because they love all. They express their love by giving what they have to someone who needs it, and they are always able to find such people in their surroundings because to them, as Maharshi Ramana said, 'there are no others'. Their life is not just long, it is also fulfilling because they truly fulfil the purpose of life.

∞

First published as a blog on 10 January 2017
Link: https://www.speakingtree.in/blog/there-are-no-others

ADVERTISING

Promoting Greed over Need

Advertising is legalized lying.

—H. G. Wells

The motive behind advertising is generally business, and the first motive of business is profit. In order to make people buy something that they do not need, it might be necessary to tell a few lies. That is why there is in the advertising industry the concept of the 'permissible lie'. In practice, a lie that is permissible is the one that is legally defensible. But the primary purpose of law is to prevent crime, not to promote morality. Spirituality goes one step beyond morality. The result is that the 'permissible lie' of an advertisement may be morally and spiritually indefensible. Here is an example to illustrate the point.

About 30 years ago, the manufacturer of a food supplement published an ad which carried stamp-size photographs of about a dozen young boys and girls who had topped in various examinations. Beneath these photographs was a statement that all these boys and girls had taken the supplement. This is a tricky ad. That the boys and girls had topped in the exams was a fact. That they had taken the supplement was also a fact. The ad did not claim a cause and effect relationship between the two facts. But an average reader is likely to deduce a cause and effect relationship, viz. that taking the food supplement had led to the brilliant academic performance. Now let us see why this deduction is invalid. The data in the ad is grossly incomplete. If we collect data on all the candidates took those exams, there will be a large number of students who did extremely well but had not taken the food supplement, and also a large number of students who had taken the food supplement but fared very badly in the exams. Therefore, the conclusion drawn from the ad by the average reader is unscientific. The conclusion may be unscientific, but why is the ad morally unacceptable? There are sure to be a large number of readers who can afford the newspaper or magazine in which the ad appears, but cannot afford the food supplement. They would be left with a sense of guilt that they are not doing the best for their children, all the more so if their children are not doing well at school. I am pleased to say that following my intervention, the manufacturers of the supplement agreed not to repeat the advertisement.

The first motive of business is profit, but it need not also be its last. The purpose of life is spiritual growth, and that is true for those in business as well as for those who create or publish ads. When we do something that blatantly contradicts the inner voice that tells right from wrong, we suffer spiritual decay. Is making a profit worth it at the expense of losing one's soul?

∞

First published as a blog on 25 May 2014
Link: http://www.speakingtree.in/public/spiritual-blogs/masters/self-improvement/advertising-and-spirituality

APOLOGIZING

Saying Sorry

Never ruin an apology with an excuse.

—Kimberly Johnson

'I am sorry' is what we tell the children in kindergarten to say every time *we* think they have made a mistake. We expect that is how they will learn to say 'I am sorry' when *they* think they have made a mistake. Saying sorry is more than good manners; it implies also *feeling* sorry. Without feeling sorry, saying it is meaningless. It also implies a sincere resolve not to repeat the mistake. And, saying and feeling sorry have spiritual implications. But these three simple words 'I am sorry' remain all our life among the most difficult words to utter. Let us examine the different types of situations which call for these words.

Accident

Occasions that call for an apology may arise as a result of an accident. We did not mean to harm anybody, but we literally step on somebody's toes by accident. The other person feels the pain, and we feel sorry that he has pain, even more so because the pain is because of what we did, even if we did it accidentally. Feeling the other person's pain implies oneness. Feeling oneness with all is a deeply spiritual feeling because it arises directly from the spiritual worldview, which considers all creation to be a manifestation of the One.

Ignorance

Sometimes, we end up hurting or harming somebody through ignorance. We often genuinely do not know what the consequences of our actions could be, or we have, at the most, a partial or erroneous idea of what our action might lead to. If in such a case we discover that our action inadvertently hurt or harmed somebody, even though we cannot change the past, we can at least compensate for it partly by apologizing. It is much better to own up to our mistake than to use ignorance as an explanation or excuse. Long explanations hide an underlying uneasiness, and the length of the explanations does not reduce the persistent recurrence of the uneasiness. The recurrent uneasiness is because our dynamic deepest Self, called 'the psychic being' by Sri Aurobindo and The Mother, tells us simply and clearly that we have done something wrong. The psychic being is neither affected by arguments, nor uses any arguments to support its verdict.

Poor willpower

Much more common, however, is the harm that results from the gap between our knowledge and will. We know what is right, and yet we do what is wrong to avoid a difficulty, hardship or struggle; or because we succumb to a temptation or to an unfair pressure due to fear or greed. Or, like Dhritrashtra, we may not be able to muster the courage to do what we know to be right due to an emotional attachment. A common example is that we all know that using plastic bags is bad for the environment. And yet, so many of us go on using them, or at least accept them if a shopkeeper offers us one, because we get tempted by the convenience. Another example: everybody knows smoking is bad for the smoker and for others around him, and yet so many go on smoking. *Gap between knowledge and practice is a universal human failing; people differ from each other in degree rather than kind.* If this gap harms somebody, we can at least apologize. But a genuine apology would be to build our resolve and do what is right the next time a similar situation arises. Both the apology and the resolve make us feel better because we are giving a partial expression to the voice of the psychic being. But the greatest joy and lasting mental peace come only from conquering our weakness and doing what is right on the next occasion.

Perverted will

Finally, we may inflict harm wilfully to secure an unfair advantage, to get sadistic pleasure or to seek revenge. In these cases, saying sorry would be pure hypocrisy unless there has been a genuine change of heart. And, if there is a genuine change of heart, then saying and feeling sorry is not enough; we should also say 'I apologize', and try our best to make amends, to compensate for the harm done. Wilfully inflicted harm has behind it a low level of consciousness. But the important point is that the level at which we are today need not be the level at which we stay forever. Rising in consciousness is possible, and is the very purpose of life. Every evil act calls for an apology, and even more than that, a resolve to improve. Not doing something evil consciously raises the consciousness and gives us joy and peace of mind apart from fulfilling the purpose of life. That is why nobody is beyond redemption. Every sinner has a future, a future that is better than the present—for him and for others. But for that, he has to make some effort; Divine Grace will do the rest.

Closing thoughts

Apologizing is difficult, but once done, it brings a sense of immense relief. Apologizing is an important step towards spiritual growth. Even if we do not accept spiritual growth to be the purpose of life, apologizing gives us joy and lasting mental peace, which we are all looking for; spiritual growth would occur anyway, irrespective of whether we know about it, want it or care for it. Thus, apologizing does more good to us than to the person to whom we apologize.

Why something that brings joy and lasting mental peace, and helps us mend relationships should be so difficult is primarily because of the ego. It is the ego that makes us view apologizing as humiliation. *Apologizing needs humility but is not humiliating.* Apologizing is an act of courage, and its effect is uplifting. Apologizing is more difficult, and therefore needs more courage, if the apology has to be offered to a child or someone junior to us in position. But at a certain level, we are all equal irrespective of age or position. And being human, parents sometimes punish their child, teachers may scold students, and seniors may pull up juniors for the wrong reasons. If a sincere and humble apology is offered to someone younger or in a subordinate position, it is not only more uplifting, it is also an extremely good and uplifting example for the younger person; it may help him pass on the act to his children, students or subordinates.

A married person soon learns that it is much better and easier to apologize than to argue, even when the person is right and the partner is wrong. Therefore, married life is a good field for learning to apologize. With apologies to Alexander Pope, to err is human, to apologize, divine. Thus, marriage helps us manifest our divinity.

∞

First published as a blog on 12 January 2017
Link: https://www.speakingtree.in/blog/saying-sorry-656540

ARMY

Forces Human and the Force Divine

An army of principles can penetrate where an army of soldiers cannot.

—Thomas Paine

Spirituality is about universal love, whereas the army is about love for one's own country, and that implies hatred at least for the enemy country, if not for all countries other than one's own. What then would the army have to do with spirituality? Some would even say that spirituality would weaken the army by making it love the enemy. This contradiction would be true if the army were a collection of unfeeling and unthinking robots, as uniformly alike as their uniforms. But the army is actually full of human beings, as vulnerable to feelings and as diverse in their thinking as any other collection of human beings. Therefore, spirituality is as relevant to the army as the rest of us; in fact, army life exposes the soldiers to situations that compel psycho-spiritual transformation if there is an opening for such a change.

Uncertainties of life

Imagine a soldier who has come home on a fortnight's holiday to celebrate with his family a festival or a wedding. Before the event, his leave might be cancelled because he is required at the border. As he leaves home, neither he nor his family can be sure if they'll even get to see him again. To live with such uncertainties with any semblance of equanimity is almost impossible without the inner strength that spirituality alone can give; if and when such an unforeseen unpleasant situation does materialize, spirituality can enhance this inner strength in not only the soldier but also for the rest of the family.

Uncertain outcome

The Gita tells us not to be attached to the outcome of our efforts because the outcome is not in our hands. But most of us find it easy to ignore this caution because we are ordinarily able to frequently ensure the outcome of our choice. For a soldier, the outcome of his efforts for him personally is always uncertain. Whether he will emerge from it alive, maimed, a prisoner of war or a martyr is something over which he has little control. But even the overall outcome of the war is somewhat uncertain. History has examples to show how the outcome has been determined by harsh climate or an outbreak of malaria rather than by the strength of the army. Realizing one's helplessness is a great stimulus for getting closer to the One Power who is behind all happenings, whose Will always prevails in the long run, and for whom, nothing is impossible and everything is very easy.

Close encounters

To the civilians, the enemy country may be little more than an outline on a map that symbolizes a group of people whose evil and recalcitrant ways have forced us to wage a war against them. The soldier, on the other hand, comes face to face with some of these people. He finds them as human as his own countrymen, with similar aspirations and preoccupations. That is why, while remaining loyal to their own countries, there might be an intensely human encounter between two enemy soldiers. For example, when faced with a dying enemy who is begging for a sip of water, an 'enemy' soldier might offer him a sip from his own precious supply of water before doing him in. To find in those against whom we are prejudiced a mirror in which we can see our own reflection is a great step towards seeing the One in all. Seeing all as a manifestation of the Divine, and living this Truth, is an unmistakable sign of perfection in spiritual life.

Disaster relief

The army not only defends our nation against enemy forces, it also plays a vital role in disaster relief within the country. That is where the compassion that the armed forces have developed through their spiritual growth finds its full expression. And, as happens with all acts that are inspired by love, the acts stimulate further spiritual growth. The commendable role that the army played in rescue and relief work in the deluge in Uttarakhand and the floods in Kashmir is recent enough to be vivid in our memories.

Closing thoughts

The fragile, futile and flimsy nature of life comes alive to a soldier with a clarity only few others can experience. Realizing the utterly temporary and unpredictable nature of life breeds love and intimacy, and encourages forgiveness. This is what spiritual growth is about. That is how a soldier grows spiritually, although he may not call it so. What name we give it is immaterial; it is the process that matters. And the process of spiritual growth or growth of consciousness is built into the job of the soldier.

∞

First published as a blog on 4 October 2016
Link: https://www.speakingtree.in/blog/forces-human-and-the-force-divine

BUSINESS

The Business of Business

No good man ever became suddenly rich.

—Syrus

The very business of business is to give less and get more; the difference is called profit. Although this in-built imbalance is legally and morally valid, can there be anything spiritual about it? Going by the general principle that all life is an opportunity for spiritual growth, business is the businessman's opportunity. To use or waste the opportunity is still up to the businessman. Let us see how.

Which business?

Will it meet a real need? Will it meet a need of the needy? Will it promote health, morality, development—something positive—or will it cater to the negative tendencies of man? Does it involve producing something or providing a service, or does it involve merely speculative buying and selling?

How to look at the customer?

Is the customer a bag of money from which we have to squeeze out as much as possible, or is she giving us an opportunity to serve, and thereby providing us an experience for spiritual growth?

The commitment

Is our commitment only to the customer or to the shareholders or to the society at large? Therefore, is it enough to provide goods and services at a low price or to give a good return to the shareholders, or do we also have to take care that our business does not deplete or pollute the environment?

Creating the work environment

Are the worker's needs and helplessness to be exploited, or do we see him as a manifestation of the Divine like ourselves, and therefore love him as a child of the same God, and therefore as a brother?

Attitude to work

While at work, are we conscious of being instruments of the Divine? Are we grateful to the Divine for giving us the talents, abilities and circumstances that enable us to do the work? Are we conscious of the unseen hand without which we cannot succeed? And if we do not succeed, do we see also in our failure the seeds of something greater, higher and wider?

Dealing with rival companies

Do only we have the right to be in the business in which we are? Can we alone meet all the world's needs? Does the world not have enough for everybody's needs, although not for everybody's greed? Isn't collaboration more productive than competition?

Taxes

While paying taxes, do we pay as much as we should, and do we pay it happily? Why should we expect a lot from the government without making a contribution? Should we not help the government in creating the infrastructure that we need? Should we not help the government achieve a certain degree of equality and social justice? How can it happen unless those who are in the business of making profit relinquish a part of the profit for the country that gives them so much?

Profit: how much and for what?

How much profit do we expect, and how do we use it? Are we content with reasonable profit; or do we exploit the ignorance or helplessness of the customer, or a high demand-supply ratio to fleece the customer? Having made the profit, do we treat ourselves as owners of the wealth we generate or do we treat ourselves as its trustees? Do we realize that making money is also a talent given by the Divine to very few, and are we grateful for it?

Responding to ups and downs

How do we respond to a windfall and a setback? Both are common in business, and both are opportunities— opportunities for spiritual growth. If it is unexpected steep progress, do we realize that it is not fully deserved? Are we conscious of the fact that many others, equally talented and hard working, achieve much less? If so, do we see the love of the Divine behind it? Further, to express our gratitude for getting more than we deserve, are we ready to share the fruits of our success with those who are less fortunate? And, If we suffer a setback, do we see behind it also the love of the Divine, who is giving us a clue as to which way life should go henceforth? Moving closer to the Divine is a gain for which no material loss is too big a price.

Closing thoughts

The above discussion raises plenty of questions but gives few answers. Yet, everybody knows what the answers should be. In other words, the knowledge for making the right choices is within us. The knowledge for making the choices that will lead to spiritual growth is within us. Why we fail so often to make the right choice is because of the pull of various temptations. Our intellect gets overpowered by our lower nature and gives us reasons for not making the right choice. The emotions and the intellect make so much noise that the shy and faint voice of the deepest Self gets masked, and we ignore it. By ignoring it, we may gain money, power, name and fame. But by ignoring it, we lose peace of mind. With each wrong choice, we take one step backward. With each wrong choice, we move one step further away from the goal of life. Spirituality can be brought into every business. Practising spirituality is the best business of all. Give all you have, expect nothing and get everything.

∞

First published as a blog on 19 September 2014
Link: https://www.speakingtree.in/blog/the-business-of-business

CELEBRATIONS

Permissible Excess

Imperfect is the joy not shared by all.

—Sri Aurobindo (*Savitri*, Book 11, p. 687)

We celebrate all occasions on which we are happy, or are supposed to be happy. The occasions may be personal such as birthdays and marriages, or public such as festivals. Even if we are the type to whom all days are alike, we do not always have a choice whether or not to celebrate. If somebody wishes me, 'happy new year', I can't say 'so what?'. But we have considerable choice in how we decide to celebrate the occasion. *All choices in life can be broadly classified into two: choices that raise consciousness; and those that lower it.* The same applies to celebrations.

Occasions that call for a celebration are bright sparks in an otherwise monotonous life. Although, in general, moderation is the best principle, an occasional excess is considered permissible. Hence, celebrations become an excuse for indulging in excess. That is where the general principle that every choice that we make either raises our consciousness or lowers our consciousness becomes relevant. *A feast is as much an excess as a fast.* Spending money to get a film star's company on your special day is a celebration, and spending the same money to give children in an orphanage a good time is also a celebration. The freedom from stereotypically civil behaviour granted on Holi can be an excuse for hooliganism and also an opportunity for rebuilding broken relationships.

Nishadbanu Vajifdhar felicitated on her wedding eve 75 teachers who had taught her from nursery onwards, and her family also donated ₹10 lakh to schools where she had studied. Two IAS officers, Ashish Vashisht and Saloni Sadana, spent only ₹500 on their wedding, the amount spent being the court fee. On the occasion of his son's wedding, Gopal Vastapara used the money that he had saved for the wedding to fund the marriage ceremony of 100 girls from economically weaker families. Manoj Munot, a businessman, spent the money that he had saved for his daughter Shreya's wedding on gifting homes to 90 underprivileged families. Both father and daughter decided to use the money differently.[1] These are some striking examples of choosing to celebrate a once in a lifetime event by an act that would raise the consciousness.

Celebrations are happy occasions. The way we celebrate reflects the type of choices that make us happy. The joy

---

[1] Pal, Sanchari, '#WeddingGoals: 11 Indian "Weddings with a Difference" We All Should Be Cheering', *The Better India*, https://bit.ly/3RAyrMT. Accessed on 14 July 2022.

of giving feels better than the happiness of receiving. A celebration designed for individual happiness can never give the joy that comes from sharing the happiness with others, especially when sharing involves giving to those who need it. We all have some creative ideas about unconventional ways to celebrate special occasions. To translate the ideas into action, what we need is the courage to be assertive with our near and dear ones without being offensive, and not bother about 'what the people would say'. Those who will laugh at us do not matter; those who matter will appreciate us. Who laughs at us and who appreciates us really does not matter. What matters the most in the long run is what effect the choice has on our own consciousness. Or, to put it in Mother Teresa's words, 'In the final analysis, it is between you and God. It was never between you and them anyway.'

∞

First published as a blog on 3 January 2017
Link: https://www.speakingtree.in/blog/permissible-excess

CONFERENCES

Conferences and Spirituality

Reading maketh a full man; conference a ready man; and writing an exact man.

—Francis Bacon

A conference does not have to be on spirituality to become a spiritual activity. Organizing a professional conference or meeting on any theme has one basic aim—sharing. For the organizers, it is hard work, but they do it so that a large number of their colleagues can meet and share knowledge and ideas with the ultimate aim of faster and better growth of knowledge in the discipline, which in turn would contribute to making the world a better place to live in. Nothing can be more spiritual than working selflessly for one's fellow beings. Nothing shared is more productive than knowledge and ideas. What a great opportunity for spiritual growth for the organizers as well as the participants! But like many other opportunities that we get in life, this opportunity can also be wasted because material and mundane motives may overshadow the spiritual possibilities.

Organizing the conference can become a fundraising event, and the funds collected may far exceed the requirements of the conference. The funds may then be used for hiring an event organizer, thus passing on the hard work involved to somebody else. Drawing up the programme can become an opportunity for pleasing as many important people as possible, so that one can later draw upon the goodwill built up to secure favours. The result is that instead of getting just a few good speakers and giving them enough time to share their knowledge and wisdom, the programme gets cramped with slots as small as 10 minutes so that nobody who matters or could matter is left out of the list of speakers. The result is that a lot of money is spent on funding the travel and hospitality of a very large number; the speakers who could give a lot to the participants do not get enough time; and snippets of wisdom get diluted by a large amount of mediocre stuff.

The speakers also have the choice of using the opportunity to grow spiritually. The presentation may begin with a silent prayer. The prayer shouldn't be for a brilliant performance, a performance which so impresses the audience that it leads to invitations to still more conferences. The prayer should be, and the speaker should mean it, for the strength and ability to speak in such a way that the people who have assembled to listen to him gain something from what he says. If he speaks with the intention of giving the audience a valuable message, a memorable learning experience, not only will the audience benefit, the speaker would also grow spiritually. But if the speaker uses the opportunity primarily to impress the audience or comes so ill-prepared that he ends up delivering a thoroughly disorganized deluge of half-baked ideas, he cannot grow spiritually through the opportunity. Besides his responsibility to the audience, the speaker also has a responsibility to the other speakers. His slot may be too short to do justice to his topic. It is also true that lesser the time available to speak, more is the effort required to prepare for the talk. But the speaker generally knows how much time he will have when he accepts the invitation to speak. If he is not satisfied with the time allotted to him, he can refuse the invitation. But to say yes, and then use the privileged position of being on the podium to go on and on beyond the allotted time is unfair to the other speakers who have to speak later in the day. Spirituality goes beyond fairplay, but it also includes fairplay. As a manifestation of the Divine like me, the other person is also at least my equal. Spiritually speaking, he is worthy of my love as a brother; if I deny him fair treatment, nothing can be more unspiritual.

The participants also have to make the choice whether to attend the conference, or to skip the sessions and go away for sightseeing and shopping. The attendance of the participants is often sponsored by their employers, and it is expected that what they learn at the conference will help them improve their work. To treat the conference as a paid holiday is, therefore, wrong. And, doing anything wrong leads to spiritual decay.

In short, as in everything else in life, so in organizing, speaking at or attending a conference, there are choices to be made. There are choices that are right, which lead to spiritual growth; and there are choices that are wrong, which lead to spiritual decay. The wrong choices are often tempting and can also be rationalized. But that does not make them the right choices. The spiritual approach is simple. The organizer, the speaker and the participant at the conference have all been given some talents by the Divine and some circumstances which have put them in those positions. They are in a position of giving and receiving love. The organizer expresses the love for the speaker by giving him an opportunity to speak. The speaker expresses his love for the participants by making a sincere effort to impart the best of knowledge and wisdom in the most effective way he can. The participants are the recipients of the love of the organizers as well as the speakers. Receiving love is also a means of growing spiritually. Receiving love involves humility. Receiving love involves transcending the ego. In case of a conference, for example, it involves acknowledging that I do not know everything and may learn something from the speaker. Receiving love gives an opportunity to somebody else to give love. Giving that opportunity consciously out of love is also an act of love. Through giving and receiving love, we grow spiritually. We can only give what we have, and only to those who need it. A conference creates an opportunity where that type of a fit exists. That is why it is a great opportunity for fulfilling the purpose of life. But like all opportunities, it can be used, it can be wasted or it can be abused. The choice is still ours. God gives us nuts and also the nutcracker, but still we have to wield the nutcracker.

∞

First published as a blog on 25 September 2014
Link: https://www.speakingtree.in/blog/conferences-and-spirituality

CONVERSATION

Spiritually Speaking, Speaking Spiritually

A man's character may be learned from the adjectives which he habitually uses in conversation.

—Mark Twain

Man is the only animal that talks and he makes rather lavish use of this unique ability. He talks, although all that he talks is seldom necessary. And he talks, although it is talking that often gets him into trouble. Sometimes he talks to people and sometimes he talks at people. It is only talking to people that is called a conversation. Our relationship with our fellow beings is a part of spiritual inquiry. The answer to the inquiry is that our fellow beings are, like us, a manifestation of the Divine. Therefore, they are our equals, and as manifestations of the Divine, also worthy of our respect. In simpler words, our fellow beings are children of the same God as we, and are, therefore, our brothers and sisters. This applies also to the people we talk to.

What?

The quality of a conversation is said to depend on whether it is about ideas, events or people—in that order. Conversation about *people* is considered inferior because it generally consists of criticism behind their back. Gossip, the favourite pastime of so many, is just that. How can talking ill of a brother or sister be spiritual? Equally bad is talking endlessly about oneself, because it is an expression of our egoistic separation from others and not that of our spiritual unity with them. Conversation about people can have a spiritual character only if it expresses genuine love and concern for the person who we are talking about. Conversation about *events* hardly serves any purpose. Talking about the implications of the events, their impact on society and so on is also a popular pastime, but it is almost like talking about the weather: nobody does anything about it because everybody thinks that nothing can be done about it. Conversation about events can become meaningful only if the persons talking about it can do something to mitigate the adverse impact of what has happened or have the capacity to influence future events in a more desirable direction. The quality of conversation about *ideas* would depend the most on the motive behind the conversation. If the motive is to exchange opinions in order to reach a less erroneous opinion, a wider and more comprehensive opinion, the conversation will elevate the consciousness of all involved. But if the motive is to get an ego boost by impressing others, it will lower the consciousness of the speaker.

How much?

In general, the less one talks the better. Most of what we talk is totally unnecessary. On top of that, conversation is between two or more persons. Therefore, apart from the general principle of talking less, it is also important to keep in mind how much time others have. Further, the conversation should follow a pace that allows a fair exchange between the participants. To hog more than one's share in the conversation is also inconsistent with the spiritual worldview. Spiritually speaking, others involved in the conversation are my equals. If I monopolize the conversation, it is like treating them as inferior.

How?

How a person talks reflects his level of consciousness. The quality of the conversation goes beyond the beauty of the language. That the language should not be crude or abusive is basic. But not listening carefully to others while insisting that others listen to us is also bad. Although it is not expressed so clearly, it is common for a person to pretend as if he is listening while actually being busy thinking of what he will himself say as soon as the other person finishes. If he waits for the other person to finish, even that would be at least something. What is worse is that he interrupts the other person, without as much as an apology. When the conversation is about a subject about which opinions can differ, sticking to one's honest opinion based on a strong conviction is acceptable, but to insist that our way of looking at the subject is the only way to look at it is unacceptable. What is spiritual is to defend the other person's right to differ even if we do not agree with him.

Closing thoughts

It may look that all these things are for kindergarten children, and bringing spirituality into the topic is far-fetched. One only has to watch discussions on Indian TV to see how much of so many of our educated eminent persons occupying important public positions actually practise what they should have learnt in kindergarten. They interrupt each other with impunity, the person who is interrupted refuses to get interrupted, and what you have are two persons shouting. It doesn't matter that nobody can understand what they are saying, but at least they have the satisfaction of speaking! As to spirituality, we boast of being a spiritual country. While we are the cradle of the highest spiritual wisdom in the world, it is the implications of the wisdom in daily life that make it of real value in making the world a better place to live in.

∞

First published as a blog on 7 November 2014
Link: https://www.speakingtree.in/blog/spiritually-speaking-speaking-spiritually

DINK

Double Income No Kids

The soul is healed by being with children.

—Fyodor Dostoyevsky

Staying voluntarily childless because both partners are working and think they do not have the time and energy to look after children is becoming a common phenomenon among the educated high-income urban elite in India. Career is important to both of them and keeps them so busy that they may not really have the time to think much about anything else. When they do have a little time or manage to 'take a break', it is to escape for a few days to Goa or Bangkok, where fun, frolic and shopping occupy their time, and they return from the break broken and broke rather than refreshed and restored. The feverish pitch of activity starts settling down only when they are nearly 40, but then it is too late to have kids.

While not having children if one does not have the time to look after them is a sensible and responsible choice, there are two questions that must be considered. First, whether raising children is a waste of time; and second, what it is that one does with the time that one has.

Are children a waste of time?

Biologically, children are a replacement for those who die; and since everybody dies one day, children are a necessity for the survival of the species. Psychologically, children give us a long-term project in which we instinctively invest a lot of time, effort and feelings, and thereby children give us something to look forward to in life. Spiritually, children are an opportunity for the parents to express love by giving. Expressing love by giving what one has to those who need it is a major route for fulfilling the purpose of life. Parents have the capacity to love and the means to express the love through care—and children need both. Thus, there is a perfect fit between what parents have and what children need. Further, giving to children is easy because nature has ensured that parents are happy to give anything to their children. In short, children provide the parents an excellent opportunity to fulfil the purpose of their lives. That is why those who stay childless often feel as if something is missing in their lives.

Apart from the above reasons, for the privileged sections of the society, having children is also a social responsibility. Most DINKs are privileged and can afford to take good care of children. If those who can give well-nurtured citizens to the country stop having children, the future citizens will be those who did not have a good upbringing because their parents were poor and uneducated. This type of imbalance exists anyway because the affluent and educated tend to have fewer children than the underprivileged, whereas logically it should be other way round. DINKs make the imbalance worse.

What does one do with the time one has?

Time is a resource with a perfectly equitable distribution: everybody has exactly 24 hours in a day. How we balance the conflicting claims on time is up to us. Time and again, the lesson that mankind has learnt is that moderation is a golden principle to follow in life. These days it is called work–life balance. To devote all of one's time to work, and that too work which is motivated primarily by monetary profit, is a highly unbalanced use of time. In the corporate sector, where so many of the DINKs work, the rule these days is to be on duty 24 hours. Even while at home, the person is expected to respond to e-mails and SMS immediately. This leaves little time for a healthy lifestyle, leave aside family and children. That is why many decide to not have children. But the results of this unbalanced lifestyle are often marital disharmony, burnout and a mid-life disease such as high blood pressure or diabetes by age 50. On top of that, the work involves coming up with tricks that befool the customers, berate colleagues, beat rival companies and cheat the government. This may lead to profits which justify the handsome salary (or 'package') of the employee, but it leads to his spiritual downfall, which is just the opposite of what the purpose of life is about. The spiritual downfall is not without its emotional cost, and that is what leads to the need for anti-depressants and sleeping pills. On the other hand, spiritual growth, which can also result from giving one's love to children, gives immense joy and lasting mental peace.

Is it always wrong to have no children?

There can be no absolute rule about anything in life. Both partners may be working, may also have a good work-life balance, and yet may decide to have no children of their own because they want to adopt one or more children. Thus, they have children, although not biological. From a spiritual angle, taking good care of adopted children is more uplifting and serves the purpose of life even better.

There is also another pattern fast emerging although it is still true of only a minority of young people. Highly educated and well-meaning young people, usually with an affluent ancestry, are taking a deeper look at life and deciding to bypass or quit lucrative jobs to do something for society. The issue that they take up may be concerned with children, women or the elderly; with corruption, education or poverty—the pet issue differs with the individual, but what they all want is to see a change in society, and for that, they are willing and happy to give up many of the so-called pleasures of life. They may decide to work with NGOs, launch their own NGOs or start a business designed to help rather than earn. In many cases, such couples are also deciding to have no children, biological or adopted. They want to spread their efforts thinly to help large numbers rather than make two or three decades of life revolve around a few children. We are all made differently, and the choice of these couples needs to be respected. They also give what they have to those who need it, and thereby fulfil the purpose of their lives. Obviously, these couples do not make much money. We may call them LINKs (Low Income No Kids). They are truly linked to the masses around them.

(Related essays: 'Grihastha', 'Parenting')

DIVORCE

The Future Tense of Marriage?

In every marriage more than a week old, there are grounds for divorce. The trick is to find, and continue to find, grounds for marriage.

—Robert Anderson

So common has divorce become in some parts of the world that there is a joke that when a schoolchild was asked the past tense and future tense of marriage, he replied that the past tense is 'engagement' and the future tense is 'divorce'. But all the same, in no part of the world is divorce a pleasant experience. In fact, it ranks among the top traumatic events that a person can experience in life. The surest way to prevent divorce would be to not get married. But that is no solution. In spite of unhappy marriages being far more common than happy marriages, the institution of marriage is nowhere near extinction. So, let us see if something can be done to reduce the risk of divorce.

Marriage rests on three pillars: intimacy, sharing and commitment. Intimacy and sharing are expressions of love. Without love, commitment is also a torture and not always worth it. Hence, the one indispensable factor that can save a marriage, and make saving it worthwhile, is that the partners should love each other. Whether the partners fell in love before they got married, or got married and hoped that they would fall in love, does not make much difference. The important thing is that falling in love can be a good beginning, but is inadequate to ensure a good ending. Let us see what a young boy means when he tells a girl that he loves her. What he means is that he is very happy in her company. It is the happiness that *he gets* in her company that makes him feel that he is in love with her. If *she also gets* a lot of happiness from his company, she also feels that she is in love with him. The illusion of being in love lasts for a while and may even culminate in marriage. But suppose she does not get any happiness from his company, and therefore thinks that she does not love him. So, she rejects him. He tries to please her, plead with her, impress her and tries all the tricks of the trade. If she still does not reciprocate, he starts getting angry with her and shouts at her, 'Why can't you see how much I love you?' In some cases, if she continues to spurn him, he may hit her, rape her or even murder her. This behaviour violates a basic principle of love: one does not hurt the person one loves. Then, why does he hurt her? Because he never loved her in the first place. He was concerned with the happiness *he gets* from her. He was not bothered about whether she got any happiness from him. Since he wanted primarily his own happiness, *he loved himself, not her*. This became apparent when she refused to give him that happiness. Love is about making the object of love happy. If he truly loved her, he would have realized that she would be happy if he leaves her alone. To make her happy, he would have left her alone; he would have never even thought of hurting her. It is because of this fallacy that this phase of 'love' is called *falling* in love. True love is not about getting something from the other person; it is about giving. This is the first shock that threatens a relationship. When partners realize that the relationship demands giving, and they are unwilling to give, there is trouble. Without giving, there is no true love, and the off-shoots of love, such as intimacy and sharing, also vanish even if they were there during the phase of the illusory love called 'falling in love'. Falling in love is not love; it only looks like love.

Hence, the first thing that reduces the risk of divorce is the willingness to give. One thing that partners these days do not give each other enough of after marriage is time. Once married, they think that the relationship has been sealed. Secure in the safety of the seal, they think now they can take each other for granted. Career becomes their top priority. So, they have no time for each other. No time means no intimacy and no sharing. They start growing distant and aloof from each other; then they start fighting. They start believing that they made a mistake; they are incompatible. Instead, they should take intimacy and sharing to a new level. That would take love to a higher level. From the phase of wanting happiness from the other person, the couple should progress, if not to simply giving, at least to give and take. After a tug of war, most marriages do settle down for a long lacklustre phase of give and take.

But the tug of war kills the love. There is so much each can do for the other: for example, one earns the bread, the other takes on the major share of parenting. What they can do for each other becomes so much of a preoccupation that there is no time to take a break from the humdrum routine. Decades pass like that, without taking a pause to ask, 'Where has the initial romantic love disappeared?'

This phase that demands give and take is also typically the phase when divorces happen. At the root of the trouble is an imbalance: one partner mainly gives and the other goes on taking. Being human, one person finds it difficult to go on giving without getting much in return. And many marriages survive only till one person is ready to go on giving without expecting anything in return. Why does that happen? That happens because most marriages start on an unequal footing. One of the partners has richer or better educated parents; or is himself or herself better educated or better looking or earns more, and so on. The result is that, to start with, one of the partners becomes the dominant partner and the other the submissive partner. In conventional patriarchal societies, it does not even need a reason for the wife to be the submissive partner. But this imbalance should not last too long. The sooner the equation is balanced, the better it is for the health of the marriage. If the imbalance goes on too long, what keeps the partners together is commitment, which is nourished by their families, societal norms, financial dependence and, above all, the welfare of the children. But a marriage in which one of the partners continues to be submissive and the other dominant, is never a happy marriage. In societies where divorce is not considered too abnormal, sooner or later the unhappy marriage ends in divorce. The confrontation, statistically speaking, comes after 12 years and two children. Who precipitates the confrontation? Who walks out of the marriage? Surprisingly, it is the partner who was submissive for so long. She says to herself, 'Enough is enough. I can't take it anymore.' And then she confronts the partner. He says, 'How dare she?' And, the stage is set for divorce. What the partners may miss is that divorce has a long background. The dominant partner was insensitive, and the submissive partner let the tension simmer for too long. It is the long-standing pent-up tension that explodes, sometimes after a relatively minor provocation, and leads to the first confrontation. That is why, if the couple goes to a counsellor, the counsellor first tries to help them develop a deeper insight into their relationship, tries to help them rebalance the equation, even if it is rather late. In some cases, it works and the marriage may be saved.

Are there some situations in which even the counsellor does not try hard to save the marriage? In two situations: extramarital relationships and domestic violence. In case of extramarital relationships, if it seems to be a one-off aberration, and the guilty partner is repentant, apologizes and promises not to repeat such a thing again, the counsellor tries that the marriage be given one more chance. But if infidelity shows a recurring pattern, even the counsellor does not try to repair the wound. In case of domestic violence, if the boundary of verbal violence has been crossed, it cannot be ignored. Physical violence is unacceptable, period. In case of physical violence, the chances of saving the marriage are bleak even if the guilty partner apologizes and promises not to repeat the behaviour because the promise is seldom kept. It is better to part ways before violence becomes regular, severe and recurrent.

From the above account, it may seem that either the marriage settles down in a dull routine, or ends in disharmony which may eventually lead to divorce. These two possibilities do cover most marriages but they need not. The third possibility is that at least one of the partners may use the opportunity provided by marriage for spiritual growth, which is possible in all circumstances including all marriages.

If the marriage is happy, or at least successful, the partners may move from the phase of give and take to that of giving for the joy of giving. This shift is usually triggered by a crisis, such as an accident, serious illness, bereavement or loss of job. The crisis makes the unaffected or less affected partner forget themselves. The other person's sorrow no longer remains that of the other person alone. One is keen to give whatever it takes to reduce the partner's suffering without expecting anything in return. Love enters the marriage once more, but it is just the opposite of what it looked like when they had just fallen in love. While then it was about getting, now it is all about giving. Therefore, moving into this phase of love may be called 'rising in love'. 'Rising in love' is spiritual growth, which is the purpose of life.

If the marriage is unsuccessful, it is actually easier to see the marriage as an opportunity for spiritual growth.

Seeing the Divine in the partner whom one does not like, seeing the hand of the Divine behind the marriage, realizing the value of not being dependent on the partner for one's well-being, all contribute to spiritual growth. Last but not least, realizing that the unhappy marriage was responsible for discovering the spiritual path which made the person's happiness independent of all external circumstances makes the partner look like a blessing. Thus, what looked like a tragedy in life is transformed into the best thing to have happened in life. The partner who looked like the person responsible for the tragedy becomes worthy of gratitude.

If divorce becomes inevitable, along with it come many tests and trials. Each test is a golden opportunity for spiritual growth. Can one go through divorce without bitterness? Can one rise above the calculations of monetary gain and loss? Can one resist the temptation to influence the children against the partner? Can one refuse the temptation for revenge? Can one resist the temptation to compete with the partner in being mean? These are only some of the tests. If both partners are able to pass these tests, which is very rare, the divorce can be amicable and short. It may be followed by a friendship that survives the divorce, and the adverse effect on children is minimal. Most important, both the partners grow spiritually through the experience. If only one of the partners has the consciousness to see the divorce as an opportunity for spiritual growth, for that partner the tests become more testing. What makes it even more difficult for this partner is that her parents, friends, well-wishers and, last but not least, her lawyer tell her not to let him off easy. The lawyer teaches her many 'permissible lies'—'everybody tells them,' she is told. The lies are calculated to create more trouble for her partner and to extract more money from him. If she refuses to fall in line, she is considered not good but stupid. Nobody understands that she is following her inner voice, the voice of her psychic being. Nobody realizes the value of the mental peace that she is getting by listening to that voice. Nobody can see the spiritual growth she is experiencing by paying heed to that voice. Everybody around her can only calculate the amount of money she is losing. Everybody around her wants her to be happy. She also wants to be happy. But the criteria of happiness differ with the vision, the consciousness, of the person involved. Divorce can be simple but seldom is because of the complications that the partners and their well-wishers can so easily manufacture. It is catering to these complications that can make the divorce yet one more missed opportunity in life.

Does it mean then that one needs to just give in and accept the divorce on the partner's terms? No, all that it means is that higher aims should not be sacrificed for the sake of material gains. In many cases, putting up a fight is necessary for the sake of the higher aims. In those situations, fighting is a sacred duty. The spirit in which the fight should be put up is best understood from the Gita. Arjun is told to fight to protect the society from evil and injustice. Similarly, the divorce should be fought to protect the society from evils, such as dowry, infidelity and domestic violence. If every woman just gives in and simply moves out, the message that goes out is that men can get away with anything. Therefore, every woman who puts up a fight is making a small contribution towards curbing social evils. In the Gita, Arjun is told to fight without attachment to the outcome. The woman should do the same. That is possible only if, as an individual, she is ready to forego the material gains. Her motive for the fight is higher; her motive is to fight social evils; her motive is impersonal. In the Gita, Arjun is told to fight without hatred for the enemy. Divorce should also be fought without hatred for the partner. That is possible only if she can see the Divine even in the partner who has been the source of so many of her problems. With this attitude, she can forgive the partner. This is not only for the sake of being good or spiritual. It is in the person's own interest to fight the divorce in this spirit. Hatred and negativity would only make the divorce painful and prolong the agony of the marriage well past the divorce. The painful bitter memories will become recurrent and agonizing. After the divorce, life with the partner belongs to the past, but the partner continues to make the person miserable by remote control, as it were. The way to deny that power to the partner is to handle the entire affair in a spiritual manner. Thus, as in all aspects of life, spirituality can purify a divorce and make it a part of the chequered vehicle given to us for going towards the goal of life.

DRIVING

A Smile Every Mile

The one thing that unites all human beings, regardless of age, gender, religion, economic status or ethnic background, is that, deep down inside, we all believe that we are above-average drivers.

—Dave Barry

Driving is an interaction. It is an interaction between the driver and the vehicle. It is an interaction between the driver and the other users of the road. It is an interaction between a man with a powerful, potentially dangerous machine at his command, others who have similar machines and also many others who don't. All interactions test how far we can put into practice what we know is the right thing to do. Spirituality is about knowing, doing and, finally, being what is right. Hence, every interaction is an opportunity for spiritual practice.

Interaction between man and machine

Spirituality acknowledges the all-pervasive presence of the Spirit of the Divine. Thus, man and machine have one fundamental thing in common: the Spirit of the Divine. Having something in common breeds intimacy and love. Hence, the interaction between man and machine can grow into a loving relationship. The interaction between the driver and the vehicle are just one example of the man–machine or mind–matter interaction. The car cannot respond to love the way a human being does, but it does respond. That is why it runs better and lasts longer in the hands of a driver who handles it with love. However, all love should be without attachment. Therefore, a scratch on the car does not justify flying into a rage and killing the motorcyclist who did it. The motorcyclist is also a manifestation of the same Divine, a child of the same God and, therefore, a brother.

Interaction with other drivers

The man behind the wheel has at his command a very fast-moving heavy machine, which is potentially dangerous. To reduce the danger, there are rules of the road. But rules spell out only the minimum expectation for preventing head-on collisions, outright chaos and traffic jams. Spirituality goes beyond rules. For example, if somebody behind me has hit my car lightly at a red light because of his inability to stop in time, poor judgment or a mental preoccupation, there is no rule that compels me to put the person at ease by looking back and giving him a reassuring smile that says, 'doesn't matter, it's okay'. A few other examples of real situations of the road follow.

There is a car ahead of me. This car can run just as fast as mine. The prescribed speed limit is 60. The driver in the car in front is driving at 60, or maybe 58. How pleasant it can be for everyone on the road if I stay behind this car, drive at his speed and maintain a safe distance. Overtaking in this situation is more an expression of my ego rather than a necessity for saving time. If I stay behind him instead of overtaking him for another 10 km, not overtaking him will delay me by not more than 10 minutes; perhaps not even that, because there may be traffic lights on the way, which are a great equalizer. Suppose I am egoistic enough to try to overtake this car. What is the best that the other driver can do? If my overtaking him is absolutely unsafe, he should give me a signal to hold on. If it is reasonably safe to overtake, he should remove his foot from his accelerator, so that his car starts slowing down, making it easier for me to overtake him in less time. But suppose his ego also starts asserting itself and he presses on his accelerator even harder to make it difficult for me to overtake, driving turns into a race. Having such a race is dangerous for both of us, for other users of the road, and also not good for anybody's blood pressure. A race track is also a road, but not every road is a race track.

The principle of being in a queue applies even to driving. If somebody is ahead of me, it is his right to stay ahead of me, unless our natural speeds are very different and it is safe to overtake. A queue signifies equality, and so does spirituality. Spirituality acknowledges the universal presence of the spirit of the Divine. The spirit binds all of us and equalizes all of us. It is a paradox that the queuing habit is conspicuous by its absence in India, a country that takes pride in claiming to be a spiritual country.

But suppose the vehicle in front of me is a three-wheeler, a TSR (taxi, scooter, rickshaw), commonly called 'the auto'. It has been designed to have a speed much slower than a car. But if the road is narrow, instead of honking and making life miserable for everybody on the road, it is better that I drive the car patiently at the speed of the auto till it is safe to overtake.

Thinking of others, which is what spirituality is about, also applies to the auto. If he finds me behind him, he should make way for me to overtake him as soon as an opportunity presents itself. If the road is wide, he should not drive in the fast lane. And if there are several autos around, which is very common, they should stay one behind the other. Instead, what they do so often is compete with each other, and the fastest among them starts competing with the cars. The result is that, quite often on a wide road on which traffic can flow very smoothly, traffic is held up because there are four autos, one almost next to the other, competing with one another, none of them really succeeding in quickly overtaking the others, but all of them together very successfully blocking at least two lanes.

Even on eight-lane highways, on which there is enough room for everybody, it is so common to find slow vehicles in fast lanes and fast vehicles in slow lanes, making avoidable switching of lanes a necessity. On top of that, there are always a few reckless drivers who assume that all the rules and speed limits do not apply to them. They are the lords of the road, who brush past every vehicle from any side they please, flitting from one lane to the other like an agile snake without even as much as an indicator, with single-minded dedication to the one objective of leaving all others behind.

The indicator is not only meant to announce the intention to turn, but also the intention to drift to the right or to the left. The indicator is not meant only to make your turning easier and safer; it can also help somebody else slow down in time or not slow down unnecessarily. The indicator may also help a pedestrian waiting to cross the road. If your indicator tells him that you will turn before you reach him, he need not wait for you. On the other hand, if he waits for you unnecessarily, he might have to wait also for another three vehicles which have now caught up and are dangerously close to him. Therefore, out of consideration for others, giving an indicator ahead of turning or drifting should become a habit which comes into play without having to think.

Interaction with the weak

Our character is judged best by how we behave with those in a weaker position. Suppose I am driving on a major road, and there is a driver coming from a small lane on my left. He wants to enter the main road. Just a little slowing down on my part and perhaps added to that a wave indicating to him that he may start moving, can make it so much easier and safer for him to merge. Another example: suppose I am close to a crossing which does not have a traffic light; there is no traffic policeman either, and I have to go straight at this crossing. There is a driver on the opposite side of the road, who has to turn right at the same crossing. He is already at the crossing, but it will take me another few seconds to reach the crossing. One way to deal with the situation is that I slow down a bit, wave to him to tell him that he may start turning, and as he turns we exchange a smile. Another way is that I start flashing my headlights, blow my horn and press on the accelerator to speed up aggressively. I scare him, make sure that he waits for me, and if there is any evidence of his being not adequately scared, cowed down and respectful, I shout at him. Yet another example: I am fast approaching a vehicle which is in a very awkward diagonal position, perhaps due to a mistake the driver has made, or because he is pulling out of a parking lot. All I have to do is to slow down, stop at a distance that leaves enough room for him to straighten his car, and then we can both start moving. Another way is to honk, abuse and brush past him on his left or his right as I feel like doing, leaving him stuck in that awkward position, making it necessary for many behind me also to deal with the same situation. Worse still, if I cannot brush past him because there is just no space, I still come dangerously close to him, and finally come to a halt in such a position that it is impossible for either of us to move. Then I start hurling my choicest invectives at him while a traffic jam builds up behind both of us. I leave it for you to judge which of these alternatives befits the residents of a country that considers itself the spiritual guru to the rest of the world. In all these situations, all we have to remember is that today it is the other person, tomorrow it may be me in the weaker position.

A person driving a car is in a privileged and sheltered environment compared to so many users of the road who are much more vulnerable. Suppose I am in a car, and ahead of me on a narrow road is a two-wheeler, and on the pillion is a precariously balanced woman having a baby in her lap. Shouldn't I be patient in overtaking them, if at all I have to overtake, instead of creating unnecessary panic and risk for the threesome ahead of me? With a little quirk of fate, the woman riding the pillion could have been my sister or daughter, and in a spiritual sense, she is, because we are all children of one God. Another situation, which almost everybody in a car has faced: at a traffic crossing, the light is green, I have to turn left, but I have just ahead of me a poor man on a bicycle with a few gas cylinders on the carrier who has to go straight, and he is pedalling hard so that he can go past the crossing before the light turns red. I have to turn left, and therefore I am at the extreme left of the road. He has to go straight, but since he is a cyclist, he is also at the extreme left. How rude and unspiritual would it be if I overtake him, and get in his way while turning left? It would be much better to slow down to his speed, let him stay ahead of me, let him negotiate the crossing before me, and then I can turn left slowly and gently, saying a prayer for a brother of mine who is breathlessly lugging such a heavy load.

Last but not least, the ubiquitous pedestrians. It is the relationship of the pedestrians to the vehicular traffic on

Indian roads that brings out the unspoken rule, 'might is right'. Let a lone pedestrian wait at a zebra crossing for eternity, and no vehicle will stop for him. But if it is a group of 20 pedestrians, they can cross the road anywhere at any time with their eyes closed, and the vehicles will have to stop for them. But God save the old man in this group of 20 if he cannot keep pace with the rest. Instead of the vehicles waiting patiently to let him also cross, they will make sure that he is made perfectly conscious of him being an intolerable burden on earth.

Closing thoughts

A celebrated quote of Sri Aurobindo is that 'All life is yoga'. What it means is that all life gives an opportunity for the practice of yoga. To elaborate further, every situation in life can be handled in a way that is yogic or un-yogic. The yogic approach is to follow some basic principles, which we may call shastra. If shastra has no advice to offer, or if one is not sure about the shastra being appropriate in a particular situation, then it is best to follow the inner voice emanating from the soul. Driving is also a part of life and is no exception to the general principle. The shastra for driving are the rules of the road. In general, they should be followed, except when breaking a rule is safer or better than following it. But, there are so many situations on the road for which a rule is not available. In those situations, the inner voice emanating from the soul tells us clearly what the right thing to do is. The right thing to do is based on love for others. Giving and receiving love are both basic needs, both give us joy and both can lead to spiritual growth. But giving love is enough. When one person gives, another naturally receives. So, let us focus on giving, and receiving will take care of itself. Let us give way, give thanks and give a smile every mile as we drive.

∞

First published as a blog on 22 June 2017
Link: https://www.speakingtree.in/blog/yoga-on-the-road

ENTERTAINMENT

Enjoy Yourself

The relaxation should be into force and light, not into obscurity and weakness.

—The Mother

'All work and no play, makes Jack a dull boy', says a well-known proverb. Its immense popularity may imply that the sentiment it expresses is beyond discussion. Although there are some people who have work that they enjoy so much that for them the division between work and play does not exist, most are not so fortunate, and for them a break from the monotony of work seems to be a necessity. When they have the break, they try to fill it with things that they really enjoy, think they will enjoy or imagine they will enjoy because others seem to. From the spiritual angle, all activities can be divided into just two categories: those that raise our consciousness and those that lower it. Since the purpose of life is to rise in consciousness, only those activities are desirable that raise our consciousness. Does this general rule apply also to relaxation or entertainment? As in all other activities, the effect of entertainment on consciousness depends not so much on 'what' as on 'how'. There is a story of two friends who decided to spend a few hours on a holiday on a relaxing activity. One of them said, 'There is a discourse by a spiritual teacher today, let us go there.' The other one said, 'At exactly the same time, there is also a Bharatnatyam recital, let us go there.' Each tried to persuade the other to go where he himself wanted to go, but failed. They parted amicably, but each went his way. The one who went for the discourse kept imagining the fun that his friend was having and regretted not having gone for the dance. The one who went for the dance kept blaming himself for his poor taste and regretted not having gone for the discourse. Thus, they both returned home feeling drained rather than relaxed. Instead, they could have both concentrated on what they were attending rather than envying the other, and enjoyed the activity. However, there is also a third way. Before the activity began, they could have both prayed for the speaker or the dancer so that he or she is blessed to do their best. 'Let the speaker get the best of ideas and the best ways to express them, so that the audience gets the maximum from the discourse,' one of them could have said. And the other one could have prayed, 'Let the dancer do her best so that the audience gets not only entertained but also feels inspired by the performance.' During the discourse, the one attending it could have been attentive, so that he could bring some more love and compassion into his life. During the dance, the one attending it could have admired the perfection in the subtle movements of the eyes of the dancer and felt the wonder of the variety of emotions the dancer could express without saying a word. All perfection carries an imprint of the Divine, and he could have connected with the Divine in the dancer that made her movements so graceful, harmonious and expressive. At the end of the discourse or the dance, both could have thanked the Divine for giving them an opportunity to grow spiritually through the experience, and for creating persons like the speaker or the dancer who can bring so much joy to so many. In short, how an activity undertaken to relax the mind affects our consciousness depends on what our attitude to the activity is rather than what the activity is. Having said that, there are crude and vulgar forms of so-called entertainment, which by no stretch of attitude can lift consciousness. Therefore, while some form of relaxation—be it change of work, a hobby or entertainment—is not a sin, a conscious choice to go for something that is uplifting is a part of walking the spiritual path.

∞

First published as a blog on 30 April 2016
Link: https://www.speakingtree.in/blog/enjoy-yourself-628442

FORGIVENESS

To Forgive Means to Forget and to Give

To err is human; to forgive, divine.

—Alexander Pope

To forgive is to forget and to give; to forget the hurt and to give love. Forgetting and loving are like two sides of a coin. Unless one forgets, it is difficult to love; unless one loves, it is difficult to forget. Genuine forgiveness is not easy. What passes for forgiveness is usually a pragmatic compromise, good manners, frustration or fatigue resulting from sustained hostility, or simply the blunting of hostility with the passage of time. Forgiveness is most difficult when hurt is inflicted by someone very close to us, and that too because we have been misunderstood. Forgiveness is not easy because a bruised ego is difficult to heal unless the ego itself is dissolved. There is only one thing that can dissolve the ego, and that is the warmth of love. Forgiveness rooted in the ego: 'I am better than the other person because I have forgiven', is not genuine forgiveness.

Forgiveness is important because anger harms most the person who is angry. The harm is physical; the person may get high blood pressure, peptic ulcer or insomnia. The harm is emotional; the person feels drained. The harm is mental; the person loses the capacity to concentrate and to think clearly. The harm is spiritual; the person hits a roadblock on the path of spiritual progress.

The ultimate antidote for all anger, resentment and hatred is forgiveness. Nobody can change the past. Nobody can change others. It is relatively easier to work on oneself. Inner work undertaken with a positive attitude is sure to yield enough ground for forgiveness. The inner work can be at the rational level. At the rational level, one can find many reasons to explain the other person's behaviour. The explanations may reside in the person's background, limited understanding (whose is not?), or in our own behaviour and outlook. Better than work at the rational level is inner work at the supra-rational level. First, the person whom I am angry with is also a manifestation of the Divine. Seeing the Divine in him is difficult, and therefore a challenge. Overcoming the challenge is an opportunity for spiritual growth. Therefore, instead of being angry, I should be grateful to the person for providing me an opportunity for spiritual growth, which is the very purpose of life. Second, the hurt and the setback this person has caused me is an opportunity for introspection, for reflection, which can also lead to spiritual growth. For example, if this person has humiliated me, it gives me an opportunity to put myself in the shoes of all those who are being humiliated day in and day out in the world, without any hope of recourse or retaliation. Feeling what they feel is itself spiritual growth, and reinforces my resolve not to humiliate anybody. There is a natural tendency to thank those who boost our egos. But those who bash up our egos deserve our thanks even more because their contribution to our spiritual growth is greater. Thus, genuine forgiveness is rooted in gratitude. It results from the realization that the objects of our anger or resentment have given us some of the best opportunities for spiritual growth. The realization makes it easy to forget what they did, and to love them instead.

It is difficult enough to rise to the level of consciousness that makes forgiveness easy. But it is vastly more difficult to stay at that level of consciousness. To make it a little easier to stay at the level of consciousness at which forgiveness comes naturally, some practices may help. One of them is the fire ritual. Write down all the resentment you have, resolve to replace resentment with love and forgiveness, and then burn the paper on which all the negativity had been expressed as a symbol of rooting it out of the system. Another way is to meditate, and during the meditation, visualize the person whom you dislike. Think of at least one good quality, or virtue, that this person has. Meditate on this virtue. Then visualize this person walking towards you and you offering the person a flower with a smile. The person is astonished, because he never expected it from you. But see the way he grabs this opportunity to make amends and becomes so sweet to you. When you come out of this meditation, you are equipped to forgive. You are ready to face this person and turn a new leaf in your relationship. During the meditation, you offered him a flower; when you meet him, you are ready to offer a hug. It is that simple. To forgive is difficult; but forgiveness can be simple.

∞

First published as a blog on 3 May 2016
Link: https://www.speakingtree.in/blog/forgive-forget-give

GAMBLING

Gambling Is Not a Gamble

Gambling: the sure way of getting nothing for something.

—Wilson Mizner

Gambling ruined the Pandavas and Kauravas, and continues to ruin lives even today. Then why do people gamble? We do what makes us happy, or what we think will make us happy. Where does the happiness of gambling reside, and how can we look at it spiritually?

There are two sources of happiness: getting and giving. We are happy when we get a new dress, and we are happy when we give clothes to charity. The joy of giving feels better than the happiness of getting; that is why it is called joy and not just happiness. When a person pursues the happiness of getting, he thinks of himself. When a person experiences the joy of giving, he thinks, at least a little bit, of somebody else also. Thinking of oneself is based on each individual being separate, which is a lower-order reality. Thinking of somebody else is based on a sense of interrelatedness, which is a higher-order reality. Wanting to get is an expression of division, wanting to give is an expression of oneness. Spiritual growth consists of moving from a sense of division to the perception of oneness.

Gambling takes the sense of division to an extreme. Each player in the game of gambling contributes to create a common pool. Each player hopes that he will be able to get from this pool more than he has contributed. Getting more than he has contributed can only be at the expense of somebody else's contribution. Wanting to get what belongs to somebody else is theft. Thus, gambling is disguised theft. And how does the person want to get what does not belong to him? Not by working hard for it, but by chance favouring him. He prays for luck. He wants to bend even the Divine in his favour. If luck favours him, he is happy. That his happiness depends on somebody else's sorrow is not his concern. If luck does not favour him, he is sad. Knowing that his loss has made somebody else happy is also not his concern. Deriving happiness from an action that is calculated to make someone else unhappy is selfishness carried to its extreme.

Gambling is a putrid passion and unbridled greed. A gambler expects luck to compensate for his laziness. Luck being unreliable, the gambler ropes in deceit. All this, to wrest wealth from others. Ramana Maharshi said, 'There are no others.' To the gambler, besides himself the world is full of others who exist to satisfy his greed. Anything that takes us away from the idea of oneness towards division leads to a fall in consciousness. Anything that leads to a fall in consciousness takes us away from the goal of life. This is true for the gambler who wins and the gambler who loses. Therefore, irrespective of the outcome, gambling wastes life. Gambling literally signifies an uncertain outcome. But the outcome of gambling is absolutely certain; the outcome of gambling is *always* a wasted life. Therefore, gambling is not a gamble.

∞

First published as a blog on 22 April 2017
Link: https://www.speakingtree.in/blog/gambling-is-not-a-gamble

GOSSIP

No GOSSIP: Go Silent, Settle in Peace

To gossip about what somebody is doing or not doing is wrong. To listen to such gossip is wrong. To verify if such gossip is true is wrong. To retaliate in words against a false gossip is wrong. The whole affair is a very bad way of wasting one's time and lowering one's consciousness.

—The Mother

Gossip is a favourite pastime and seems harmless. This harmless sentence makes time look like a problem and gossip an enjoyable solution. Time is a precious resource to be used, not a problem to be solved. That is point number one. And gossip is not harmless. As Sri Aurobindo says, 'Chat of that kind has indeed a very tiring effect...because it dissipates the energy uselessly.' That is point number two.

What do people gossip about? The list is endless, but one popular topic is 'people', and generally it consists of talking ill of somebody behind her back. This is the worst type of gossip and lowers consciousness the most. The person who talks ill of somebody knows that it is wrong and risky, and that is why she also tells the person who is listening not to tell anybody else. The listener is made to feel privileged because she is the only person in the world with whom this 'fact' is being shared. But the hope that a 'secret' shared will stay a 'secret' generally does not materialize. It gets shared with more and more, one by one, and each person with whom it is shared feels equally privileged. Finally, the secret is widely known and may eventually go full circle to reach, after getting considerably spiced up through each transmission, the person who gave it away the first time, or even worse, the very person who was criticized. It is said that once a friend of Socrates was very eager to tell him something about somebody who they both knew. Socrates interrupted him, and asked, 'Are you absolutely sure that what you are going to tell me is true?' The answer was 'no'. Then Socrates asked, 'Are you going to tell me something good about the person?' The answer was again 'no'. Finally, Socrates asked, 'Will what you tell me do some good to me?' The answer was again 'no'. Socrates ended the conversation by telling his friend, 'Then please do not tell it to me.' Listening would have done Socrates no good but some harm, and to the friend who was going to tell him still more harm. What type of harm? What can be worse than wasting the non-renewable resource called time, and in this case, the wastage would have been made worse by lowering of the consciousness; the two together are a disaster.

Another much-loved topic for gossip is 'events', national and international. Generally, this type of gossip is full of criticism of leaders and governments. Since we criticize people who are remote or organizations that are nameless and amorphous, we think it is safe and harmless. Further, we feel that by criticizing the people who we think have created all the problems, we have solved the problems of the world. There can be no worse illusion than this. The gossip session is over, and nothing has really changed. The eloquent speaker has only given his ego a boost by showing his 'unmatched and unprecedented' understanding of issues, and by indirectly hinting how all the problems of the world would disappear if only he (and those listening to him) were put in the place of the stupid bunch that rules the world. What we forget is that problems will disappear only when the consciousness of the human race goes up, not by a change of leaders or governments. Giving the ego a boost is a sure way of lowering the consciousness. Thus the gossip, by lowering the consciousness of everybody involved in the gossip, has actually brought down the average level of consciousness of the human race, thereby adding to the problems of the world!

The gossip that can be looked upon rather charitably is that about 'ideas', especially ideas that are the ideals of mankind. When these ideas are the subject of gossip, the speaker touts them as his opinions. First, seldom is anybody's opinion truly his own. What we think is our opinion is a synthesis of what we have picked up from many sources over a long period of time. Second, the speaker feels good about having such grand opinions, and his capacity to express them so effectively. That is again an ego-boosting exercise. Finally, if others also participate in the gossip by expressing their opinions on the same topic, there are sure to be differences which could occasionally end in an avoidable conflict. The conflict is often due to each person's ego asserting itself by defending its own position rather than due to one person being right and another being wrong. Truth comes in shades of grey rather than black and white, as Niels Bohr said, 'the opposite of one profound truth may very well be another profound truth.' For example, the Isha Upanishad (verse 5) says, 'That moves, and That does not move'—two opposite expressions, and yet both are profound truths. Hence, conflicts due to differences of opinion about grand ideas are generally a reflection of ignorance, or at best partial knowledge. No words can express the total truth, because words are finite while total truth is Infinite.

There is one variety of 'gossip', which may be called 'silent gossip', the internal contradiction notwithstanding. We often talk to ourselves, going over events of the past, daydreaming about the future, sometimes even having imaginary conversations with people. This variety may waste only our own time and lower only our own consciousness. But that is an important enough reason to stop even such 'silent gossip'. This type of gossip gives verbal expression, although we do not vocalize it, to thousands of thoughts that have a way of invading the mind every minute. Much of thinking is unnecessary, and so is much of speaking, whether aloud or silent. This is the principle of the mindfulness type of meditation. Mindfulness basically means being mindful of what the mind is full of. It is not enough to practise this discipline only during meditation; it should have a spill-over effect. This type of self-imposed discipline should become a habit and extend to the whole day.

Finally, one 'gossip' that might be condoned is *sharing to unburden* oneself. A person going through a difficult phase of life might look upon being with a friend as an opportunity to feel lighter by talking about her problems. This might end up being an informal counselling session. While such sessions can be a valuable support in bad times, the person in whom we confide should be chosen carefully. This person should be a true friend who is also a good listener, and should, at that moment, have the time to listen to us. Further, this person should be neutral and objective in his perception in spite of being our friend. This person should also be one whom we can trust to keep secrets. Finally, it is desirable also that this person is wise enough to give some meaningful advice. The best advice would be one which helps us go through the difficult phase of life with minimum suffering and maximum spiritual growth. If you do not have even one such person in your life, take heart in the fact that you have plenty of company. Most of us are all alone in a very crowded world full of 'relatives and friends'. That is why professional counsellors fill a real need, although they may charge us for their services. But there is One Counsellor who is available to each of us, to the rich and the poor alike, any time of the day or night, without an appointment, completely free of cost. You know whom I am talking about. As The Mother has said, '...the best friend one can have—is he not the Divine, to whom one can say everything, reveal everything? ... He is the true friend, the friend of good and bad days, the one who can understand, can heal, and who is always there when you need Him.' However, to be able to get the best from this Counsellor, we should contact Him regularly, even on good days.

Gossip: what a harmless little luxury, and even that is being snatched away you might say. Spirituality is about giving up small luxuries, and gaining the big ones. It is giving up our dependence on small comforts like gossiping, and getting the comfort of the lap of the Divine instead. It is about getting liberated from our bondage to small pleasures, and getting the Joy that does not bind. Liberation (*moksha*) is what we all want, and spirituality brings it to us, without our having to die. Or one might say, we have to die to our old self, and be born to a new Self, to experience *moksha* in this very life, in this very world.

(Related essay: 'Conversation')

GRIHASTHA

Bringing Spirituality Home

The advantage of growing up with siblings is that you become very good at fractions.

—Robert Brault

Grihastha (*griha*: home; *stha*: stationed in) is the phase of life (roughly age 25–50 years) when there is no getting away from home or the domestic responsibilities that go with it. In traditional Indian wisdom, it is the second of the four phases of life, each about 25 years long. The phase before grihastha is brahmacharya (birth to age 25; the learning phase), and the ones that follow grihastha are vanaprastha (age 50–75 years; the phase of getting detached from family life) and sanyas (age 75 years onwards; the phase of total renunciation).

Some historical factors, which we need not go into here, implanted about a thousand years ago in the Indian psyche the idea that the ordinary householder's life is one type of life for the masses, and the spiritual life is another type of life for a select few. This dichotomy is artificial. Not only can spirituality be brought into domestic life, without spirituality domestic life becomes a burden, it degenerates, and life may be left with no higher purpose than feeding and breeding—something that animals also do. It is true that one can rise to a level much higher than that of animals exclusively on the basis of rationality, but that is much more laborious and risky, and also eventually becomes a backdoor entry into spirituality.

Does spirituality require leaving home?

No, home is a part of our circumstances. Circumstances are the vehicle available to us in the journey of life. The path that the journey follows depends on the goal, not the vehicle. The goal of life should be, according to The Mother, high and wide, generous and disinterested. This is an excellent description of spiritual growth. If spiritual growth is adopted as the goal, any circumstances, including those of a householder's life, can be used for going towards that goal.

How can spirituality be brought into domestic life?

Spiritual growth requires rising above our little self. Ego is the barrier that makes us obsessed with that little self. Love is the antidote to ego. Love for the family is instinctive, and therefore family life is an easy way to embark upon the path of spiritual growth. The ideal of the spiritual path is love without attachment. The family is the field available to most of us for most of our lives for practising love, but it is accompanied by attachment. The knowledge that love brings joy and attachment brings sorrow is helpful. But the knowledge becomes real to us only when our own experience confirms it. Therefore, one may start with love with attachment. When we face disappointments and failures within domestic life, or when we suffer due to attachments, our experience starts confirming the knowledge that attachment brings sorrow. When experience confirms the knowledge, love continues (and should continue), but the attachment goes down. Thus the ideal of love without attachment is something that is attained in steps. It is not a one-time event. The important thing to remember is that even love with attachment is better than no love at all.

Reaching the stage of love without attachment applies also to love for the spouse. If love for the spouse is coupled with attachment, one is dependent on the spouse for one's happiness. Let me explain. Well-adjusted happy couples look forward to a retired life: 'after retirement, we will have so much time, we will travel a lot, talk a lot and do so many things together', and so on. It is not infrequent that in such cases, one of the partners passes away a little before or after retirement. Now, the surviving partner is shattered.

The same thing applies to children. The child grows up and goes to another city or country for college education. The parents, particularly stay-at-home mothers, are shattered—psychologists call it the 'empty nest syndrome'.

In short, if our happiness is dependent on something that will not and cannot last, it is a happiness that is always vulnerable, always susceptible to the inevitable changes in life. How can one get lasting happiness from something that itself cannot last? And nothing in the world lasts; everything is perishable. That is why, on the spiritual path, one eventually discovers happiness that is independent of external circumstances. It is happiness that comes from love without attachment. It is happiness that is based on only one attachment: attachment to the Divine, and the Divine is everlasting. Love for the family and love outside the family are both eventually seen as love for manifestations of the Divine.

Should one have personal expectations from children?

No, each child is a distinct individual. It can neither be our carbon copy, nor is it obliged to fulfil our expectations. All that may be expected from our child is that it chooses a career and lives a life that will bring out the best in him or her for a noble use. As Kahlil Gibran said:

> *Your children are not your children.*
> *They are the sons and daughters of Life's longing for itself.*
> *They come through you but not from you,*
> *And though they are with you yet they belong not to you.*

The lack of expectation applies not only to their career but also to the common expectation that children will take care of us in old age. For a variety of reasons, at least children should never be told that this is expected of them. First, sermonizing is not good parenting. Secondly, sermonizing does not work. Finally, love coupled with expectations of getting something in return is a bad example for the child.

If even parental love is burdened with expectations, where will the child see an example of unconditional love that does not expect anything in return? All that we should work towards is making the child a good human being. If we succeed, the world will get a good citizen, and we will get a good child who will look after us in old age—but that should neither be the reason for bringing children into the world nor the covert or overt aim of parenting. The usual logic that since parents have done so much for the children, the children should do something for the parents in return is flawed logic. The children do not have to be grateful to parents. The parents should be grateful to the children for giving them an opportunity for showering their love, which in turn helped them fulfil the purpose of their lives. The children will fulfil the purpose of their lives by showering love on their children.

Just as love without attachment is one hallmark of the spiritual path, love without expectation is another. Expectation also brings sorrow, just like attachment. Sorrow may come because the expectation is not fulfilled. Sorrow may come even if the expectation is fulfilled, because the state of fulfilled expectation may not last. Sorrow can come even if the expectation is fulfilled, and the state of fulfilled expectation has not yet come to an end because of the insecurity: 'how long will it last?'

What is the next step?

To a person on the spiritual path, family life is good training. It teaches the person to love. Love breaks the ego barrier between him and the family. Breaking the ego barrier means that he learns to look at which need is more important rather than whose need it is. It is no longer my need versus somebody else's need; it is a pooling of the needs of the family, and addressing first the need that is most important. Family life teaches the person on the spiritual path not only to love but also to love without attachment. Family life teaches the person to love without expecting anything in return. Family life teaches the person to love in spite of getting criticism in return. Family life teaches the person to love even those who are unlikable. This process, however, does not have to stop with the family. After doing it for more than 20 years, the person should become an expert on love. The expert is now ready to move on to the next higher rung of love, which is to love those not related to him by blood or marriage.

Love may be extended to 'the community', that is, the people whom we know. But it should go higher: it can be extended to 'strangers'. To a person on the spiritual path, there are no strangers because to him all are children of the same God. The process of extending love beyond the family does not have to wait till all family responsibilities are over. Love for the family, and love for those outside the family can and should co-exist. Some professions have an in-built opportunity for extending love outside the family. For example, the students provide this opportunity to teachers; patients do it for doctors and nurses. By providing this opportunity, students help the teachers grow spiritually, and patients do the same for doctors and nurses. What can be better than having an opportunity for rising to a higher rung of love while still being immersed in domestic life and fulfilling the purpose of life by doing a job that also, incidentally, helps make a living. That is why these are called noble professions.

However, after the domestic responsibilities are over and the family does not need the person any more, extending love outside the family is the sole avenue available for continuing to grow spiritually. To grow spiritually, all that is needed is to be aware of what we can give, and find someone who needs it. We always have something to give—money, an object, time or at least a smile—and we can always find someone who needs it. We are not helping the person who needs it; he is helping us by giving us an opportunity to grow spiritually, to fulfil the purpose of life. That is how fulfilling the purpose of life is a life-long agenda; it ends neither with 'retirement', nor with 'getting the children settled and building a house'. Love for the family can and should evolve into love for others, but it is not an inevitable consequence. One has to be conscious of the higher purpose of life to evolve to the higher rung of love consciously. Negotiating the journey of life consciously, as in any other journey, takes us towards the goal in less time and greater comfort.

GRUMBLING

Obsessive Compulsive Complaining

Some people are always grumbling because roses have thorns; I am thankful that thorns have roses.

—Alphonse Karr

Grumbling is a habit. There is a story of a man who found faults with his wife's cooking. His wife was a good cook. She tried to cook better. The complaints did not stop. She tried hard to find what her husband's favourite foods were, and tried to cook those items as well as she could. The complaints did not stop. She tried to find out which foods her husband did not like. She stopped cooking those foods. The complaints did not stop. Finally, one day, she cooked in such a way that even her husband could not find any fault with it. That day he said, 'Why can't the food be like this every day?'

Grumbling is an obsession. Those with this obsession are always able to find something to grumble about. Grumbling is compulsive complaining. Even when the complaint has been taken care of, the grumbling does not stop. The one who cannot help grumbling enjoys grumbling more than seeing any change. Enjoying what makes a person miserable is the result of perverse thinking, or giving in to a habit instead of thinking.

Grumbling is an attitude—One that is just the opposite of gratitude. The one who grumbles has no time to see anything positive. He finds nothing to be grateful for. What a tragedy to miss the joy of gratitude for the sake of the perverse pleasure of grumbling!

All our feelings, thoughts and actions may be divided into two categories: those which raise our consciousness; and those which lower it. Grumbling lowers the consciousness, gratitude raises it. The choice is ours. If we have made our choice, we get the will to work on it. Although very difficult, it is possible to work even on attitudes. Just getting rid of a negative attitude is difficult; replacing a negative attitude with its opposite is easier. Replacing grumbling with gratitude is not easy, but it is possible. The time to begin this inner work is now.

Never grumble. All sorts of forces enter you when you grumble and they pull you down. Keep smiling.

—The Mother

HEALTHY LIVING

My Body, My Business

I get my exercise acting as a pallbearer to my friends who exercise.

—Chauncey Depew

Advice is generally resented, especially unsolicited advice. When a person is advised to eat a healthy diet or to exercise or to stop smoking, it is generally accepted gracefully but not always gratefully because some people want to go on living the way they do. Their unstated attitude is, 'My body, my business. I would much rather live 10 years less than miss my samosas and pizzas or my daily drink.' This is not a rational attitude, and certainly not spiritual.

First, the rational part. When I am sick, not only do I suffer, but so do my caregivers. If I cannot work due to the illness, the society suffers. When I get treated, especially in a government hospital, the taxpayer pays for it. When I die prematurely, the world loses what it invested in me without getting enough back. In short, a person with a chronic disease is a burden and a drain to the world.

Next, the spiritual part. I have come to this world with a purpose. The purpose is to grow spiritually, or to grow in consciousness. For that, the field that I have is life. The equipment that I have is the body and the mind. The vehicle that I have is the work that I do. If I have been given certain abilities, the circumstances to hone those abilities and the opportunities to use those abilities, the least that I can do is to take good care of the equipment. For example, a factory manager is expected to clean, service and oil the machines so that the machines go on working for a long time. In the same way, we are expected to take care of the body–mind complex. Neglecting the body is betraying the trust that has been placed in us by the Divine. Therefore, taking good care of the body is a sacred duty. If I fail to do my work properly, I lose my opportunity. For the Divine, running the world is a game. The Divine has no shortage of players to continue the game, and with eternity at its disposal, the Divine is in no hurry to finish the game.

You would say that the whole edifice is based on a certain view of life and the purpose of life defined by somebody else. Why should I accept it if I think that the purpose of life is to enjoy it? And why am I not free to enjoy it the way I like? Just a little reflection shows that the fleeting pleasures that spoil our health have never brought anyone lasting happiness. On the other hand, what one has to do to fulfil the purpose of life as 'defined by somebody else' is to live a life that is guided by love for our fellow beings. Such a life is full of joy, lasting mental peace, good health and fulfilment. These are the very things that we are all looking for anyway. Instead of looking for them in junk food or late nights, why not find them where they reside. And, to enjoy them for a long, long time, why not take good care of the body.

Does a life full of love for our fellow beings guarantee good health forever? That is not true either. Even saints and sages get illnesses, even incurable and painful illnesses, and eventually they die. But what is true is that while saints and sages get an illness, they do not suffer from the illness. Thus, what is guaranteed in a spiritual life is lasting mental peace in spite of problems, illness being only one of the problems to which spiritual life provides no immunity. If one gets peace which cannot be disturbed by pain, people or problems, what more can one ask for?

> *If our seeking is for a total perfection of the being, the physical part of it cannot be left aside; for the body is the material basis, the body is the instrument which we have to use.*
>
> —Sri Aurobindo

INTERNET

Internet Connects

Day by day, and night by night, he called up one corner of the globe after another, and looked upon its life, and studied its strange sights, and spoke with its people. ... He seldom spoke, and I never interrupted him when he was absorbed in this amusement.

(Mark Twain's description of a character using an invention, which he called telectroscope, in a science fiction story that he wrote in 1898.)[1]

The internet is incredible. What it has made real would have been dismissed as impossible even 25 years ago. Sending letters and pictures worldwide instantaneously, finding answers to questions serious or silly in a fraction of a second, banking and buying (and bullying) from home, discovering friends long forgotten—one could go on and on with what the internet has done.

---

[1] Crow, Jonathan, 'Mark Twain Predicts the Internet in 1898: Read His Sci-Fi Crime Story, "From The 'London Times' in 1904"', *Open Culture*, 11 November 2014, https://bit.ly/3uVo38O. Accessed on 18 July 2022.

But what has spirituality got to do with all this?

Spirituality is about discovering the Spirit that unites us, about love that can unite us, and expressing that love through giving, caring and sharing. In other words, spirituality is about gaining uninterrupted awareness of our inherent divinity and organizing our life around it. Such awareness or consciousness invariably reveals to us also the all-pervasive presence of the Divine. It is not only we who are inherently divine, so is everybody else. Discovering this basic identity with our fellow beings forms the basis of all of us being interrelated. Identity and interrelatedness lead to intimacy and love. But such a feeling of universal oneness requires spiritual consciousness, which is qualitatively different from the ordinary consciousness. Spiritual consciousness has been restricted so far to a select few, whom we call saints, sages and mystics. The ordinary consciousness is essentially mental, whereas mystic consciousness has access also to planes of consciousness higher than the mental. Mental consciousness is ego-driven and, since the ego is concentrated on the individual, it has a separative character. Mystic consciousness transcends the ego, perceives oneness, and thereby breaks the barrier between individuals. Breaking of the ego barrier leads to love and compassion. It is because the majority of mankind has an ego-driven consciousness that the world is a place characterized by selfishness, evil and injustice, and the consequent misery and suffering. That it has been so for thousands of years does not necessarily mean that it will always be so. We live not in a static but in an evolving universe. Evolution from matter to life and from life to mind has essentially been a gradual unfolding of the Supreme Consciousness of the Divine. The latest product of this unfolding is man. However, there is no reason to believe that evolution has stopped with the advent of man on the planet. If the trend so far is any indication, it may be safely assumed that further evolution will lead to a species that will express a still greater fraction of the Consciousness of the Divine. However, man has at least two unique characteristics. First, man has reached more or less the summit of mental consciousness. Second, man has the capacity to grow in consciousness in his lifetime and a select few have, from time to time, grown so much as to approach the highest possible consciousness—these are our rishis and mystics. Sri Aurobindo and The Mother have indicated that the next leap in terrestrial evolution is now not far away. The next leap would mean that higher, deeper and wider consciousness that has so far been confined to a select few will become commonplace. When the number of individuals with a level of consciousness perceptibly higher than the present average crosses a certain threshold, there will be much more feeling of oneness, and consequently much more love and compassion in the world. An unprecedented acceleration in the pace of evolution of consciousness has now been noted by several other modern spiritual thinkers such as Gary Zukav, David Hawkins and Nikki de Carteret. Several indicators of the revolutionary change of consciousness sweeping the world have been collected in a book titled *Enlightenment Now* by Steven

Pinker, professor of psychology at Harvard University.[2] In short, evolution towards a better world is in progress. Has the internet in any way promoted tendencies that would raise the collective consciousness of human societies?

The vastly improved connectivity involving millions of people across long distances made possible by the internet has triggered spiritual tendencies in ways more than one. First, it has made more of us more acutely aware of the diversity in appearance, language, culture, opinions and morality that exists across the globe, and also the common causes and concerns that dominate human life everywhere. Thus it has facilitated, on the one hand, acceptance of differences, and appreciation of oneness on the other. Secondly, it has facilitated rapid unprecedented global dissemination of news about extremes of good and evil. Dissemination of news about the heights to which man may rise inspires heroism. Dissemination of news about the depths of degradation to which man may sink inspires activism. Good and evil have always co-existed on earth, but never before did good react to evil on the scale that it does now. Thanks to the internet, it is just as easy to collect millions of dollars for a good cause as it is to collect

---

[2]Pinker, Steven, *Enlightenment Now: The Case for Reason, Science, Humanism, and Progress,* Penguin Random House, New York, 2018. Also see Zukav, Gary, *The Seat of the Soul,* Simon & Schuster, New York, 1989, pp. 13-21; Hawkins, David, *Power Versus Force: An Anatomy of Consciousness: The Hidden Determinants of Human Behaviour*, Veritas Publishing, Arizona, 1998, p. 67; and de Carteret, Nikki, *Soul Power: The Transformation That Happens When You Know*, O Books, UK, 2003, p. 100, p. 282.

millions of signatures to fight an evil. People scattered all over the world can unite and speak in one voice to promote love amongst people who are unrelated by clan, creed or culture. Finally, the internet has ushered in a knowledge revolution. The combination of 'professors' Google and Wikipedia has made knowledge from the trivial to the transcendent, from Bhangra to brain surgery, available to all in an instant virtually for free. Since its inception in 2001, Wikipedia has grown to be the world's largest volunteer-led project and the biggest online repository of knowledge. Almost all its content is freely available for use and reuse. Currently, there are about 300 Wikipedia in different languages, including 22 Indian languages. All these Wikipedia are hosted by a United States non-profit organization called the Wikimedia Foundation. The ethos of Wikimedia is to make 'a world in which every single person on the planet is given free access to the sum of all human knowledge'. Add to Wikipedia, Wikibooks, which aims at providing textbooks on every subject; Wiktionary, a multilingual dictionary and thesaurus; Wikivoyage, a travel guide; and Wikisource, which has out-of-copyright old books, including not only works of Shakespeare and Chaucer but also a book on Sanskrit Grammar by William Dwight Whitney, late professor of Sanskrit at Yale University, originally published in 1950 by Harvard University Press—and you have a vast amount and range of knowledge available free to just about everybody in the world. The approach of Wikimedia (WIKI) is obviously quite the opposite to that of Intellectual Property Rights (IPR). While IPR is about ownership, WIKI is about sharing. While IPR is based on mental calculations and logic, WIKI is based on the highest rung of love that emanates from the psychic being. While IPR is based on the idea that an individual created the knowledge and therefore has rights over it, WIKI is consistent with the idea of universal knowledge, for a small fraction of which the writer is only a channel. The way WIKI has grown in less than 20 years and outstripped in its range and reach the works based on IPR is evidence of the power inherent in higher levels of consciousness. And who has made WIKI and its phenomenal growth possible? A large community of individuals who have risen above their little ego-centred self to a wider all-inclusive Self. Moving from a world in which knowledge is 'owned' to a world in which knowledge is voluntarily 'shared' is one of the indicators of the movement towards a higher level of consciousness of the human race visualized by Sri Aurobindo and The Mother.

The effect of the internet has been mixed, as has been that of religion. But as in the case of religion, the overall effect of internet will also be positive, if for no other reason than that a small amount of positivity can overcome a much larger amount of negativity. That is why freely shared knowledge has been able to overshadow knowledge on sale in such a short span of time. The fact that crime, cruelty and corruption can no longer be hushed up easily is itself a major step forward. Invention of the internet seems to be a phenomenon that the Divine has devised to push humanity towards the next phase of evolution. The Divine works in mysterious ways. The internet seems to be one of the ways by which the Divine is working out the destiny of the planet.

∞

First posted as a blog on 28 August 2016
Link: https://www.speakingtree.in/blog/internet-connects

LEADERSHIP

Someone to Follow, or Something to Follow

Whatever the Best does, that the other men also do; the standard he creates, the people follow.

—The Gita 3:21

Just as there are born teachers, there are also born leaders. Observe a group of five-year-olds playing, and you will find one of them dominating and directing others as if he is double their age. And the beauty is that the others listen to him; rebellions are few and far between. But, just as teachers are also made in teacher-training institutes, there are courses and workshops on leadership. Logically, a born leader who has also undergone leadership training will be better than the leader who has only been trained. Logically, yes, but not necessarily so; in fact, the most revered and remembered leaders never underwent any leadership training. For example, which course on leadership did Mahatma Gandhi or Abraham Lincoln attend? Hence, the important point is not how one can become a leader, but why we need leaders and what makes a good leader.

Why leaders?

Heterogeneity is a fact of life. We are all equal but not the same. Some know more than others; some understand life better than others; some can control others while others need to be controlled. In short, we need a few to lead so that the rest know which way to go.

Who is a good leader?

A good leader is one who is not interested in becoming a leader. It is the followers who see a leader in him and love to follow him. The good leader treats his being treated as a leader as a privilege. He realizes that the leadership qualities have been given to him by the Divine. The circumstances that nurtured the leadership qualities have also been given to him by the Divine. The opportunity for his becoming a leader was also created by the Divine. These realizations make him humble and push him to introspect how best he can do justice to the privilege. Some of the things he does in response are that first, he tries his best to set a good example, and even more important, not a bad example. Secondly, he uses the power that he has over the lives of others to improve their lives. For example, if he is the team leader in an organization, he ensures that those working with him have a good work–life balance. And, they should not feel compelled to do anything ethically or morally wrong at the workplace. Finally, they should feel loved and respected. Love and respect are neither a courtesy nor good manners. They come from the realization that we are all imperfect manifestations of the Divine, and we are all differently imperfect. In fact, we can reduce the imperfection by seeing the viewpoint of others and making allowance for their nature. Moreover, he does not think that he is being nice to those who he is leading. He is just using what he has been given by the Divine to express his love for those who have been brought in contact with him by the Divine, and thereby living a meaningful life. He is not helping those who he is leading; they are helping him by providing him an opportunity for fulfilling the purpose of his life, which is spiritual growth. The leader might have to be, at times, strict and even impose punishment. But the followers should be able to see in that too the insight and good intentions of the leader, and the necessity and justice inherent in the action.

Closing thoughts

The Divine is the leader of the universe. Within the universe is this earth, for us the world. For our world, the goal of the Divine seems to be Its progressive manifestation through the process of evolution of consciousness. Every leader can benefit from considering how, within the limited sphere that he is leading, he can collaborate with the Divine as a willing and happy instrument. In fact, every organization, be it a nation, a company, a school or a hospital, is a mega-individual or a mini-world. It has a divine centre, a soul and the sacred responsibility of the leader is to facilitate the manifestation of the soul of the organization through the activities of its individuals and, thereby, contribute to the evolution of consciousness on the planet earth.

MANAGEMENT

Manager, Manage Thyself

For harmony and better work, it is not by changing men that things can get better, but by changing one's own consciousness and character.

—The Mother

Management, as we understand it today, is a product of the industrial revolution of the nineteenth century. Its aim is to maximize production and profits. The prevalent model of management that has evolved treats man as yet one more machine in the factory, with the only difference that man is the most difficult machine to deal with. Unlike non-living machines, man is whimsical, avoids work and has endless demands. Therefore, men are machines that have to be controlled. This gives rise to the need for two types of employees: the controlled and the controllers. Managers are the controllers, and their job is to control those working under them. The task of controlling men, who are assumed to be basically reluctant to work, needs a bag of tricks, such as 'carrot and stick' and 'divide and rule' and, if necessary, 'revenge and deprivation'. Since the basic aim, and often the only aim, is profit, the employee, including the manager himself, should be paid less than the revenue that he generates for the company, and should be paid only as long as serviceable.

How do the managers generate revenue many times their fat salaries? The top managers do it by coming up with ideas which successfully befool or cheat the customers, the shareholders, rival companies and the government, besides being ruthless with their juniors while setting targets for them. The junior managers do it by working day and night to chase the unrealistic targets, and by signing on the dotted line without thinking whom they are cheating while doing so. Subservience and selling the soul are an unwritten part of the MBA curriculum. Top management institutes teach their students: you are paid to do what you are told to do, not to think about what is right and what is wrong. This is the inside view of much of management today, which is quite a contrast with the highly competitive entrance tests for admission to management institutes and the highly paid jobs that their graduates get. It is basically money, not job satisfaction, which is driving engineers to opt for selling real estate and credit cards. Those who have the guts and the ability quit and become writers like Chetan Bhagat, or accept a salary cut to work with an NGO, or launch their own start-up with a judicious mixture of pragmatism and good intentions.

What does spirituality have to do with the above model, the prevalent model, of management? It has twofold relevance. One, neglecting the voice of the soul while making choices takes its toll on our health and well-being. That is why managers typically resort to smoking and drinking as expedients for keeping stress away. That is why by 50, so many managers experience burnout and are ready for the golden handshake. That is why by 50, most managers have one of the midlife diseases, such as high blood pressure, heart disease, diabetes or cancer. Most managers can see their future by the time they are in their 30s, but the alternative is to keep losing one job after another. That they cannot afford, because by then they are trapped. They have a family to look after, and they have got accustomed to a lifestyle that needs the fat salary to pay all the EMIs.

The second relevance of spirituality to management is to look for an alternative model of management. The best alternative is the one based on the spiritual worldview. According to Vedanta, man is basically good; each person is potentially divine. What the manager has to do is to bring the best in the person to the surface. This can be done by treating the person as if he is good. That will encourage him to bring his goodness forward. Secondly, spirituality is not against profit. But making profit is not the highest aim of spirituality. Therefore, profit has to be made within the framework of right and wrong. The higher goal is spiritual growth, or growth of consciousness. That is a goal that is common to the manager and 'the managed'. Perception of a common goal and adherence to permissible means makes everybody committed to a higher aim and faith in a Higher Power for achieving the aim.

Workers often turn against management because they are treated as tools that will do a certain job, not as human beings with thoughts, feelings and souls. Even with the best treatment, misunderstandings and dissatisfaction may be there. But in case of a conflict, the spiritual approach is to rise to a higher level of consciousness which brings forth greater love, trust and empathy. What happens more commonly is that in a conflict, both the parties sink to a lower level of consciousness, which brings forth more hatred, suspicion and indifference. Sri Aurobindo's advice to managers regarding the treatment of their subordinates is: 'To be able to see the viewpoint of others and make allowance for their nature—neither being too harsh, authoritative or exacting, nor too weak and accommodating or indulgent, but still, even when firm, combining firmness with tact and sympathy...the subordinates generally must be able to feel...that they are being dealt with in all uprightness and justice and by a man who has sympathy and insight and not only severity and energy.'

In a study on a small sample of managers on the path of Integral Yoga of Sri Aurobindo and The Mother, Larry Seidlitz found that these were managers with a difference. They encountered difficulties in dealing with people, they sometimes had doubts about their own attitudes and actions, but they could still manage successful enterprises while also taking care not to deviate from the spiritual path. The key to dealing with difficulties is to look within rather than outside in other people and circumstances. Secondly, one can go by the dictum that difficulties have a potential waiting to be released. The manager should be able to see the hidden potential and help others in the organization to see them. Summing up the advice of Sri Aurobindo and The Mother, which different managers studied by him used to varying degrees in their own way, Larry Seidlitz writes,

> ...using tact, sympathy and gentleness together with firmness; looking within for the cause of disagreements or conflicts; guiding and building up people instead of cutting them down or expelling them; and finding the proper place for people within the organization where they can fulfill their roles without coming into conflict with others. The participants also had useful suggestions: patiently explaining what needs to be done; repeating instructions and the expected standards in work as often as necessary; sympathetically nurturing and helping the personnel to develop their abilities, helping them to see both their limitations and their progress.[1]

According to Sri Aurobindo, an organization is like an individual. It has a physical part—the infrastructure, machinery, etc. It has an emotional part—the energy and dynamism. It has a mental part—its guiding principles and goals. But, most importantly, it also has a soul, a unique ideal all of its own, which facilitates evolution of the organization. An organization can fulfil itself only

---

[1] Seidlitz, Larry, *Integral Yoga at Work: A Study of Practitioner's Experiences Working in Four Professional Fields,* Indian Psychology Institute, Puducherry, 2016.

by discovering this element, pursuing it in its work and expressing it in its daily life.

One may end this essay with a comprehensive and succinct summary arrived at by Larry Seidlitz. He says that the essential principle of applying Integral Yoga in work generally is 'becoming aware of the Divine's Presence'. He goes on to say,

> The Divine's Presence is everywhere and in all things, and takes the form of the soul in each individual being and each organized group. Aligning oneself with this Divine Presence, becoming aware of it and allowing it to express itself through oneself as a conscious and collaborating instrument, is the key to progressively manifesting one's own highest unique possibilities, as well as the key for an organization to manifest its highest unique possibilities.[2]

---

[2] Ibid.

MARRIAGE

Finding Meaning in Marriage

The value of marriage is not that adults produce children, but that children produce adults.

—Peter de Vries

Marriage is an institution created by man to reconcile the desire for sex with needs that are uniquely human. Marriage makes it possible to combine sex with prolonged parenting by both parents, and at the same time leaves scope for satisfaction of the intellectual, aesthetic and altruistic needs of man. In that sense, marriage is a compromise. It allows sex, but not unbridled sex. It allows progeny, but not too many. It lets us cater to our uniquely human needs, but only within limits. Since marriage has scope for a bit of everything, rational analysis is overwhelmingly in favour of marriage. But spirituality, while not rejecting reason, goes beyond it. The question of marriage may be stated from the spiritual angle thus: 'Does marriage help or hinder spiritual growth, which is the purpose of human life?'

If we look upon life as a journey, life is the vehicle we have for going towards our destination. The vehicle in the journey of life is life itself. As long as we have life, we have a vehicle. A married person has one type of vehicle, an unmarried person another. In a journey, the vehicle has only marginal importance. If the driver knows where he has to go, even a bicycle will take him there; if he does not, even a car cannot. Going towards the destination is critically dependent not on the type of vehicle a person has, but on the choices made at crossroads and T-junctions. Similarly, life also offers us choices. To make our choices, we may make use of the guidance coming from the heart, the head and the soul. The three sources of guidance do not have to speak in different voices, but often they do. It is the soul that provides us the guidance that will take us towards the goal of life, but we have the free-will to act upon it, or to reject it.

The choices emanating from the soul are choices based on love. Love breaks the ego barrier that divides us from others. One of the corollaries of the spiritual worldview is that our separation from one another is only a superficial reality. At a deeper level, we are all one, and therefore inter-related. Love is therefore the practical expression of the spiritual worldview and makes that worldview more real to us. As the spiritual worldview becomes more real to us, our consciousness grows deeper, wider and higher. We become a different person; a more loving, compassionate, non-judgmental and all-accepting person. That is what spiritual growth is about.

A married couple makes a commitment to be there for

each other through all the ups and downs of life. They share their joys and sorrows, their fortunes and misfortunes. This comes very close to dissolving the ego barrier completely between two individuals. In the ego circle that previously had only one individual, now there are two. After they have children, the circle expands further. The love the partners have for their children is even more sincere than for each other. Love to children is given spontaneously, unconditionally and without expecting anything in return. Love for children is strong enough to survive the terrible twos and the turbulent teens. By giving up personal comforts for the children's welfare, by loving the children in spite of their mistakes and misbehaviour, by forgiving their follies, parents get good training in showering genuine love on someone who is intrinsically weaker, someone who is dependent on them. By placing the children's needs ahead of their own, parents dissolve the ego barrier between themselves and the children.

Ego expresses itself not only through catering to one's own needs, but also through sticking to one's opinions. A householder has no choice but to respect, or at least acknowledge, the opinions of not only the partner but also those of the children, his own parents and his partner's parents. Balancing and accommodating divergent viewpoints, disagreeing without being disagreeable and turning a disagreement into the best decision through discussion, all require controlling one's ego, which is the first step towards breaking the ego barrier.

Ego also expresses itself through anger. Because of intimacy, and because of a deep-seated but erroneous feeling that relationships within the family are unbreakable and therefore can be taken for granted, anger within the family is sometimes expressed in language that would otherwise be considered absolutely unacceptable. Forgiving the worst forms of anger and insults, and returning once again to normal acts of loving and giving is something that can happen only in a householder's life.

A fragile relationship can break not only through anger but also in a crisis. Within the family, someone may lose a limb, become bankrupt, get a chronic incurable illness, get paralysed or get a disabling disease like Alzheimer's, but none of these becomes a justification for breaking the relationship. Crises put the person's love to severe tests and trials because of the total commitment to the partner and the children. The commitment is only to a few, but it is total; hence, when much is asked of him without any prospects of relief or recompense, the choice is between unconditional unstoppable love, which leads to spiritual growth; and walking out of the responsibility, which leads to spiritual decay. The social and psychological bonds that make it difficult to walk out, paradoxically, carry the key to spiritual liberation. Caring for an incompatible partner, a rebellious child or a child with special needs, ungrateful in-laws, or a crippled or comatose parent, are challenges and opportunities for spiritual growth, which only a married person generally gets. The result is that after going through married life for three or four decades, people, especially women, rarely remain the same; they are invariably much better persons to whom loving, giving and caring comes much more easily. Whether the crisis is simply managed somehow, or is used as an opportunity for spiritual growth is up to each individual in the family, but a few such opportunities for taking a few giant leaps towards the goal of life invariably appear in each householder's life.

Thus, a householder's life is an excellent vehicle for spiritual growth. The only limitation is that love *may remain* confined to those related by blood or marriage, but such exclusivity is not essential. Even while a person is going through the thick of family life (grihastha), it is generally possible to shower some love on others by giving money, objects, care or knowledge. For a lucky few, such as doctors, nurses and teachers, this opportunity is built into the work that they do. Further, when grihastha is over, and the major responsibilities taken care of, the person can reach out to those not related by birth or marriage. Grihastha is excellent training for further spiritual growth, for going beyond where family life could take us. At the end of grihastha, if the opportunities offered by family life have been used well, the person is an expert in loving. The expertise acquired during the long and rigorous training as a householder can now be used for loving anyone around us, and the love expressed by giving those who need what we have—be it time, money, care or knowledge. Loving those who are not related to us by blood or marriage is a rung higher than loving those who are. We typically have about 25 years (age 50-75, vanaprastha) for walking the path of further spiritual growth through this higher rung of love. Moving from love restricted to a few towards love that is more universal in character requires overcoming attachments to relationships, possessions and work of a particular variety, which generally develop during grihastha. Overcoming these attachments is also a part of spiritual growth. Since an unmarried person may never develop such intense attachments, he is denied that opportunity. How can one overcome something that does not exist in the first place? In short, a householder's life is an excellent vehicle for fulfilling the purpose of life, first by offering opportunities for loving the family unconditionally expecting almost nothing in return, and then for offering the same type of love to many more. Divine love that a self-realized soul has is universal, unconditional and expects nothing in return. There is no bar to a householder climbing to that summit.

In short, a householder's life is packed with all the ingredients that life, as a vehicle, provides for moving towards the goal of life. Initially, it provides opportunities for growing spiritually by loving those for whom love is instinctive. Thus the process of spiritual growth begins the relatively easy way. After the person has been trained in loving those for whom love comes easily and naturally, the person can go on to the next rung of love, and express love to those who are not related by love or marriage. Thus marriage has opportunities for going, step by step, all the way in the spiritual journey that life truly is. Whether a person makes use of the opportunities or not is up to him, but he cannot blame marriage for his not making enough progress.

A classic example of a householder yogi is Lahiri Mahasaya. Having reached the summits in his previous incarnations, the role he had to play in this life was to demonstrate that a householder's life is compatible with the highest yogic attainments. He not only got married but also had two sons and three daughters, served in a government job and looked after the extended family after his father's death. The ideal situation is one in which both the partners are serious and sincere spiritual seekers. Then they can together progress faster than they would individually. Such a partnership has been termed a spiritual partnership by Gary Zukav. But like all ideals, spiritual partnerships are rare at the present level of human consciousness. What is more common is that only one of the partners is consciously interested in spiritual growth, and this partner grows partly by using the more worldly-wise partner as a challenge and an opportunity for spiritual growth. Gary Zukav, who, like Sri Aurobindo, has visualized a major leap in human consciousness in the relatively near future, has also visualized the present marriages giving way to spiritual partnerships.

Once Dilip Kumar Roy, a great intellectual with strong spiritual inclinations and a passion for music, asked Sri Aurobindo's advice on getting married, the reply that he got was, 'In your own case everything depends on your ideal. If it is to lead the ordinary life of vital and physical enjoyments, you can choose your mate anywhere you like. If it is a nobler ideal like that of art or music or service to your country, the seeking for a life-companion must be determined not by desire, but by something higher and the woman must have something in her attuned to the psychic part of your being. If your ideal is spiritual life, you must think 50 times before you marry.'

In short, for most people, the best option seems to be the good old system of 'ashramas'. During the first 25 years of life, one should get the education that prepares the person for life, not just for making a living. During the next 25, one should live a householder's life, not losing sight of the sense of right and wrong. This will lead to not only modest spiritual progress, but also train the person for making faster progress during the remainder of life. During the remainder, the person can progressively widen the sphere of one's love and weaken the ties that bound him during grihastha. The spiritual progress through this scheme may not be phenomenal, but life is likely to be happy, healthy, peaceful, meaningful and fulfilling. To live such a life successfully and to be content with it are great achievements; anxiety for spiritual progress can only make matters worse. Spiritual greed is just as dangerous as material greed. For the rare individual who is ready for a giant leap, Divine Grace will ensure that she gets the circumstances that are best for her. The Divine Grace will also ensure that she gets the wisdom to use the circumstances that she gets for phenomenal spiritual progress. As Sri Aurobindo has said, 'He who chooses the Infinite has been chosen by the Infinite.'

Opened were gates of unforgettable bliss:
Two lives were locked within an earthly heaven
And fate and grief fled from that fiery hour.

Sri Aurobindo (*Savitri*, Book 7, Canto 1, p. 468)

MONEY

Money Is Not Poisonous

Money is a means, a force, a power, and not an end in itself. And like all forces and all powers, it is by movement and circulation that it grows and increases its power, not by accumulation and stagnation.

—The Mother

Money is something funny. It is like the beautiful girl with whom everybody likes to flirt but nobody wants to be seen with. The hypocrisy associated with money explains many hackneyed phrases such as 'It is not a question of money, it is a question of principle', or 'I am not working for money—I just want to stay busy doing something useful'. When a person says, 'Money is nothing', test him by asking him to lend you some.

Everybody needs money because it can get us some of the necessities of life. The difficulty is that there is no clear boundary where necessities end and luxuries begin. However, no matter how much money one has, that does not change the fundamental principle that happiness lies in reduction of desires, not in their fulfilment. Secondly, when one has the money, one may acquire some objects of desire, but one should neither become dependent on them nor get attached to them. Dependence and attachment may lead to much suffering, if at some later stage in life one has to do without them. Finally, money can get us only some of the necessities of life; there are others that money cannot buy. For example, money can buy a bed but not sleep; money can buy food but not appetite; money can buy sex but not love; money can buy drugs but not health.

Money also gives a sense of security. That is why there is a tendency to spend less than what one earns, and save the rest for a rainy day. However, the security that money gives also needs some qualification. First, there has to be a point, of course arbitrary, at which a person has to say, 'enough, also for security'. Otherwise, fear and greed will ensure that the person is miserable all the time; he will not need an emergency to do that. Second, while money does help overcome many emergencies, it has limitations. There are many situations, especially illnesses and accidents, in which a person feels completely helpless in spite of good financial resources. Finally, the ultimate security resides in the Divine—that is the only resource that never fails us.

Besides being the means to acquire some necessities, and to give us some sense of security, what else is money? Money is also a spiritual test, both when we have too much of it, and when we have very little. If we have too much money, it does not really belong to us because the talents that enable us to make money are God-given gifts. Being able to use those talents is a still greater gift because all those who are equally talented are not equally successful at making money. As Sri Aurobindo has said, 'All wealth belongs to the Divine and those who hold it are trustees, not possessors.' If the Divine has trusted us with more than our share of the money, it is our sacred duty to use it for the welfare of those who have received less than their share. Performing this duty with the right attitude (i.e. without ego, without desire for name or fame, and with gratitude for the ability and for the opportunity to give) leads to spiritual growth and gives us a sense of fulfilment. On the other hand, if we have very little money, that is also a spiritual test. It tests whether we can still retain an attitude of contentment and gratitude. Further, if a poor person is generous towards those in need, even the little that he gives is worth more than a much bigger amount donated by a rich person to a charity.

In short, money is not poisonous, and making money is not a sin. If one has money, it should be used for transcending selfishness. Accumulating money beyond a point is meaningless. Money, by itself, is of no use unless used and circulated. Throwing away money to satisfy one's own vulgar and extravagant desires is a terrible waste of an opportunity given to us for gaining peace and fulfilment the easy way. The ancient Indian ideal says it all: pursuing worldly desires (kama) and the means to fulfil them (artha) are legitimate if the pursuit stays within the limits of righteousness (dharma) because the ultimate goal of life is liberation (moksha).

Everybody wants to grow rich,
And some really do.
But those who feel rich,
Are indeed very few.

The thrill of earning more,
Is to all so dear.
But the joy of needing less,
Is not so clear.

Earning more
Creates conflicts in the mind.
Needing less
Leaves desires behind.

Earning more may need
The conscience to be killed.
Needing less may leave
No desire to be fulfilled.

The needs are very few,
But unlimited is greed.
Greed gets its due
From ego, a wild weed.

Desire and ego:
A terrible breed.
The more you feed them,
The more they need.

No ego, no desire:
The path of sunshine
For all who aspire
To discover the Divine.

Yoga: a trying road,
Blocked by ego and desire.
Every step on the road,
Lifts a man from the mire.

The road is long,
The goal may be never seen.
But every step brings along
Joy in seasons good and lean.

Joy in every season
Has a rich feel.
Richness beyond reason,
Safety beyond a seal.

∞

First published as a blog on 27 September 2012
Link: https://www.speakingtree.in/blog/money-is-not-poisonous

PARENTING

Children Help the Parents Grow

Don't worry that children never listen to you; worry that they are always watching you.

—Robert Fulghum

Becoming a parent is considered so natural and such a necessary part of life that if a couple does not get a child within a couple of years of getting married, people they know start getting worried; if not worried, concerned; and if not even concerned, at least curious about it. Most couples also get miserable if they cannot have a child, although these days it is not uncommon to take a conscious decision to stay childless. Apart from its obvious importance for perpetuation of the human race, what do parents get from parenthood? Kids are cute, they are fun; but they are also terrible at two, rebellious in their teens and eager to leave home in their 20s. Traditionally, children have been considered a security against old age, a role that they cannot always be relied upon to fulfil. Is there something that parents get predictably and reliably from children, all the time, without fail and without any delay? Children give the parents an opportunity to love. Love is meaningless without giving. Love becomes even more meaningful when it involves giving that is difficult to give. And parenting is nothing if not going out of the way to give. For a few decades, the life of a couple revolves around their children. Typically, the father tries to generate the means for providing sustenance, education and a lot more to the child. He may sacrifice his comfort to provide better for the child. In the film *3 Idiots* when a father says that he went round on a scooter instead of a car so that he could collect money for his child's education, he is illustrating the spontaneous sacrifice that parents willingly make for their children. They may even risk their lives when the child is in danger. The mother may sacrifice her career for the sake of the child. She schedules her day in such a way that she is at home when the child returns from school, and is available to drive the child to art, dance and music classes, the swimming pool and birthday parties. She sacrifices her sleep when the child is not well. Couples who do not get along well may continue to stay together for the sake of their children.

Giving as completely, unconditionally and selflessly as parents do to their children is possible because parents treat their children not as 'others' but as extensions of themselves. In other words, the ego barrier that normally separates each individual from the rest of the creation is essentially non-existent between parents and children. When the ego barrier does not exist, the person does not think in terms of whose need it is—his own, or the other person's. He thinks rather in terms of which need is more important. If to that is added love, the other person's need invariably seems more important. Normally, love weakens the ego barrier; in case of children, the weak barrier makes love natural. Normally, mutual liking and attraction generate love. In case of children, love leads to liking and attraction. That is why parental love is unconditional. Even a child with a cleft lip is very beautiful to its mother.

Reflection reveals in this process a remarkable similarity with the love that God has for us. We are an extension of God, and thus Its children. God loves all of us irrespective of how we look or live. And God or the Divine does not expect anything in return from us; in fact, It has everything and needs nothing. That is why parental love transcends human love; it approaches divine love. Anything that makes us grow in the image of the Divine takes us closer to the Divine. Getting closer to the Divine makes us acquire the nature of the Divine. Getting closer to the Divine helps us allow the Divine to govern our lives. In other words, parenting leads to spiritual growth or growth of consciousness. And, spiritual growth is the very purpose of life. Thus, children help us fulfil the purpose of life, and thereby give meaning to our lives. This is the only thing that children always do for their parents, and nothing else is really necessary.

What if a couple wants children but is unable to get any? This should be treated not as a disability but as a blessing in disguise. This should be treated not as the lack of an opportunity for fulfilling the purpose of life but as a bigger opportunity. The couple can adopt a child. If they treat the adopted child as their own, the spiritual growth is even more than with the biological child. Spiritually, even more significant is a couple having one or more biological children and still adopting at least one child. A similar opportunity is available to step-parents.

There comes a stage, usually when the child is around 20, that the child genuinely does not need the parents much. This is the time to realize that the time has come to move on. We have fulfilled our responsibility of looking after the child. More than that, the child has fulfilled its responsibility of helping our spiritual growth, and we now need to find other avenues. Often, the child may quite willingly and happily leave home to study or work in another town, at least partly to get away from parents. Even if the parents are not ready to let go of the child, the child's behaviour invariably prompts them to. It is only because of their inappropriate attachment to the child that they may refuse to see the obvious signals. They put up with the child's wayward behaviour, continue to cling to the child and feel an emptiness in life when the child finally leaves home physically, or at least emotionally. Nature's intention behind this natural process of children distancing themselves from parents is perhaps to help the parents. The agenda of life is not over when the children are grown up. The true purpose of life is spiritual growth, and that should continue till the last breath. Having exhausted the possibilities of using children as the means of the spiritual journey, now it is time to adopt another mode of transport, a better mode of transport. Over the 20 years that parents grow spiritually by loving the children, parents become experts in loving. Time then comes to use this expertise for loving those who are not biologically related to the parents.

What love needs is a complementary situation. We should have something to give, and there should be someone around who needs it. At every stage of life, we all have something to give. After our children have left home, we may have money, an object, physical care, knowledge or just time to give. And, if we look around, we can always find many who need what we have available for giving. There are bright children whose education has been interrupted due to lack of money, and we may have the money to help them out. We may have children's books, clothes and toys lying idle at home, which many other children outside can use. We may still have the strength to help an elderly person. We may have the knowledge to teach the children of our domestic help or the children living in slums. Or we may just give time to an NGO as a volunteer to work whenever they need us. These are just examples of the avenues for spiritual growth available to us after our children do not need us anymore. These avenues will help us along the next leg of the spiritual journey because they involve loving those who are unrelated to us by blood or marriage. But at a deeper level, we are all related to one another. We came from the same Source. We are all children of the same God. We are all in this world playing different roles, and thus following different paths to progress on similar journeys with the same goal.

If children make spiritual growth relatively easy and enjoyable, are those who are somehow left childless really unlucky? A general principle of life, which can be applied without exception to all situations, is that every situation is an opportunity for spiritual growth. If we have the vision to see the opportunity, what looks like a tragedy turns into a blessing. This principle also applies to the situation of being childless. Being childless means that one does not have to spend 20–30 years of one's most productive life loving only a few, and that too loving those neglecting whom is not an option; caring for them is a social, legal and moral responsibility. A childless person, while still in his or her youth, has the opportunity to practise a higher rung of love, the rung that normally becomes available on a significant scale only in old age. Thus, being childless is a shortcut—one that bypasses the tough terrain of looking after biological children. The childless individual can straightaway shower love on those unrelated to him by blood or marriage, do it by giving what he has been blessed with to those who need it, do it when he has plenty of energy for it, and go on doing it for several decades. In short, while enlightened parenting takes a person further on the spiritual journey in a good car travelling on a pothole-ridden road, to the enlightened person, childlessness provides a supersonic jet. The key is to discover the Divine within, and let the Divine Light guide life. Then any life that we get becomes a vehicle for fulfilling the purpose of life. That is what fills life with fulfilment.

∞

First posted as a blog on 28 May 2017
Link: https://www.speakingtree.in/blog/children-help-the-parents-grow

PHOTOGRAPHY

Past Images and Future Life

Photography is an immediate reaction, drawing is a meditation.

—Henri Cartier-Bresson

In less than 200 years, photography has revolutionized our pictorial records of the past. What an artist did in hours, and still imperfectly, photography could do in an instant with amazing accuracy. But photography did not kill art because more than making an exact copy, art is for self-expression. Today, it is possible to combine art with photography to get a combination of creativity, self-expression, accuracy and efficiency. However, the advent of digital photography, with its ease and ubiquity, has also multiplied manifold the traps and temptations of relishing the past.

To bring out the contrast, let us go back to the time when photography was essentially restricted to studios, where people went once in a while, well dressed and groomed, sat like a statue, followed the instructions of the photographer about which way to look and how to smile, and then stuck the black-and-white picture in a family album. A couple of albums that the family built up served as a record of how amazingly a person's looks had changed over the years, and as a reminder of how the family had changed as a result of births, deaths and marriages. Once in a while, at family get-togethers particularly, the albums were retrieved, and viewed with nostalgic abandon and glee. Over decades, personal cameras became common, pictures became colourful, albums multiplied and started storing pictures also of friends and family trips and picnics. But the change was rather slow and more quantitative than qualitative.

Today, the phone that one carries everywhere also has a camera built into it. Pictures can be clicked on impulse, recording a video is equally easy, selfies have become the norm and sharing of pictures across long distance is very simple. There is no limitation of 'film', and the cost per click is negligible. While the widespread availability of enormous freedom and feasibility is welcome, it has also raised some new issues and magnified some issues that are timeless in character. Several emerging issues, such as the narcissism promoted by selfies, the security risks involved in sharing pictures widely, and the questionable morality and risk of blackmailing involved in pictures taken in bedrooms and bathrooms have been widely discussed. Let us focus here on the timeless spiritual dimensions of nostalgic exercises in general, with special reference to photography.

Importance of appearance

In photographs of people, the focus is on appearance. Appearance is a reality, but an inconstant reality. But each appearance or form is a manifestation of the Divine, which is constant and imperishable. What lies concealed in the form is the spirit of the Divine, which is only partially expressed in the manifestation. With time, form is expected to change anyway. The goal of spiritual progress, and the purpose of human life, is to express more of the spirit of the Divine. A greater expression of the spirit is also called rising in consciousness. Rather than be interested in how our appearance has changed over decades, the change we should be more interested in is how much the consciousness has risen over those decades. While speaking of an artist's approach to form, The Mother has said that to the artist, forms are 'the covering of something else'. His art expresses 'his relationship with the realities which are behind' the forms. That is why 'a living art' is not 'just a flat copy of Nature'. That explains why art can be potentially more spiritual than photography.

Missing the present

It is not uncommon for people to spend more time clicking pictures and videos than observing the beautiful scenery or the dance performance, or communicating with friends who are travelling or partying with them. We are more interested in the future occasion when we will be able to get a poor copy of the experience than in making the most of the present. That future occasion comes only rarely, if at all. But in the process, what we can get from the scenery, the performance or the company of friends in front of us is more or less gone. Observing the image on the screen of a phone or a tablet cannot come anywhere close to the real thing. Instead of soaking in the beauty and joy of the moment, we are engaged in a task instead of relishing the moment with a peaceful and silent mind. Spiritually, it is more important to make the best use of the present, than to think about the future. The past is dead and gone; nobody can change it. Over the future, we have, at best, only imperfect control and that control depends on how we use the present. The present is all we have in which the choices we make determine which way our consciousness, and consequently our life, goes in the future.

Attachment and narrowness

Keeping on thinking about the people whom we have known in the past, seeing their pictures and enjoying the recollection of moments we have shared with them, and reflecting over the fluctuations our relationship with them has gone through over time only intensifies our attachment to the same set of people. Some of the older relatives may be no longer around, some of the younger ones might have grown up and do not need us anymore. Some of the friends we had in the past have distanced themselves from us for various reasons, or are simply out of touch. Spirituality is not about these attachments, and remaining confined to a narrow circle. Spirituality is about expanding the ego circle.

Spirituality is about adopting as our own those who happen to be around us, and showering our love and affection on them. Spirituality is about building up partnerships based on spiritual affinity rather than on blood, marriage or shared factors such as workplace or neighbourhood. Finally, spirituality is about giving, as an expression of universal and unconditional love, what we have to those who need it. The contradiction between the attachments that photography promotes and the relationships that spirituality demands is too obvious to need any elaboration.

Living in the past

The very act of clicking is linked to an urge to cling to the past. The present is seen as superb, we know it will not last long, we do not visualize anything better in the future, and therefore we want to capture the present in the hope of reliving it when it belongs to the past. But why do we have to cling to the past? Spirituality is about progress, about moving from where we are to where we should be and can be. Spirituality is about a new birth without actually dying. How can we be born to a new Self without forgetting the little self of the past? It is no coincidence that people steeped in spiritual cultures like that of India have a poor sense of history.

Closing thoughts

Spiritually speaking, clicking pictures, storing and organizing them for easy retrieval, and going over them periodically is not only a waste of time but also an obstacle on the path of spiritual progress. Enjoying a repeat view of old pictures is a part of the common tendency to enjoy dwelling on the past. Much of the gossip at get-togethers is about the past, particularly if those who have got together are above 50. The favourite pastime of senior citizens is reflecting romantically over the past and comparing it with the terrible present. Among the *anuvratas* (small vows) in the Jain tradition, one is to refrain from enjoying past memories. A deeper reflection explains why a seemingly innocuous popular indulgence has been 'banned' in a religious tradition. The 'ban' is designed to aid spiritual progress by weakening at least one of the most difficult barriers, the barrier called attachment: attachment to form, attachment to possessions and attachment to relationships.

∞

First posted as a blog on 4 February 2017
Link: https://www.speakingtree.in/blog/past-images-and-future-life

POLITICS

Pleased to Ask You to Do as I Say

I slept and dreamt that life was joy. I awoke and saw that life was service. I acted and behold, service was joy.

—Rabindranath Tagore

Politics is a much-maligned word, but who is above politics? Man is a political animal. Politics is not just at the national and international levels, there is politics in organizations, communities and families. Very young children use their political instincts to manipulate parents. Politics is about power and control; acquiring and wielding power in order to control others. Controlling others boosts the ego. Thus, like much of human activity, politics is also rooted in the ego, which is a basic feature planted in every creature having a mental consciousness and consists essentially of exclusive concentration of an individual on the self.

Power and control are very practical entities. Since that is what politics is about, politics is a very practical activity. It has a theory, but practice deviates from theory to an incredible degree. Politics is neither about being good, nor about being intelligent; at best, it is about being wise. Success in politics also needs the capacity to befool and manipulate, tempt and intimidate. But, at the same time, the basic human urge to transcend lower nature affects politics too. In politics, this urge takes the shape of using power to solve the problems of human existence. However, man being primarily a mental creature, politics seeks mental solutions to the basic problem of inequality from which ensue injustice and cruelty, which in turn lead to much misery and suffering. Since the intellect is a versatile tool, it has approached the problem in a variety of ways. Each approach leads to a particular system of government, such as monarchy, dictatorship, oligarchy, aristocracy, plutocracy, democracy, socialism or communism. However, more than the system, it is the persons in power who have determined the success of the system in reducing misery. This happens because of two basic factors. First, all systems have a rationale, and their intentions are good. Secondly, any system can succeed or fail depending on the level of consciousness of the persons using the system to wield power. To understand this, let us take two contrasting systems, democracy and communism. Democracy lets the people rule themselves through their elected representatives. People know what is best for them, and therefore, their representatives should also know what is best for the people. Hence, the representatives may be expected to use the power that they have been given by the people to take decisions which would be good for the people in general. They should be able to ensure the largest good for the largest numbers. Perfectly rational and well-intentioned—who can have any quarrel with these basic principles? Communism allows for individual differences in temperament and abilities, but emphasizes that being human is enough to make them all equal. Therefore, they all have a right to have their basic needs met. In exchange, each individual should be prepared to do for society what he is capable of doing. Hence, the basic principle: from each according to his capacity and to each according to his needs. It is the responsibility of the State to ensure that each individual does actually contribute to the society, and that everybody's basic needs are actually met. The basic principles are again perfectly rational and impossible to find fault with.

Why do they fail?

Although their basic principles are very rational and their intentions noble, neither democracy nor communism have been able to wipe out the problems of human existence. The root cause of their failure resides in the level of consciousness of those who have implemented the systems. Since the average human consciousness is ego-driven rather than love-driven, those in positions of power, irrespective of the system, have tried to corner more than their share of resources. The result is that inequality and injustice continue, and so do the resultant misery and suffering. The three buzzwords of the French Revolution were liberty, equality and fraternity. Sri Aurobindo has pointed out that at the present average level of human consciousness, if people enjoy liberty, inequality is sure to follow, as happens in democracies. On the other hand, communism could impose some semblance of equality only by taking away liberty. Thus liberty and equality cannot co-exist. The keyword is fraternity. If there is a feeling of universal brotherhood and sisterhood, both liberty and equality would be automatically ensured. I cannot keep myself free and keep my brother or sister in chains; that ensures liberty. I cannot be well-fed while my brother or sister is starving; that ensures equality. But fraternity needs the ego barrier to be dissolved by universal love. At the present stage of evolution, the ego barrier is too real to be dissolved by noble intentions and pithy slogans.

Power is an opportunity

Having power is a pleasant experience. All experiences, pleasant or unpleasant, are opportunities for spiritual growth, which is the purpose of life. But in case of pleasant experiences, it is easy to waste the opportunity. That is why, power corrupts more often than it elevates. A person who is conscious of the purpose behind all the experiences that are given to him in life will use the power that he has to take decisions that can help those who are dependent on him, those on whose lives he has some control. One little decision by the head of the government can improve the lives of millions in the country. By taking such a decision, more than helping the people, he is fulfilling the purpose of his own life.

While the problems of human existence are unlikely to be over till the average level of human consciousness registers a perceptible upward shift, there is something that individual political leaders can still do. As and when they have power, they can use it for taking decisions that would be good for the people. Like all decisions that are truly right, these decisions will give them immense joy, lasting mental peace and a sense of fulfilment. Even more important, these decisions will take them nearer to the goal of life. These are consequences that nobody can stop, nobody can take away from them. The extent to which people benefit from their decisions, and what happens in the next election, are things that are not in their hands. But the spiritual growth that they experience, and the fulfilment of the purpose of life that they achieve, are guaranteed. It is primarily for our own spiritual evolution that we are here on earth, and the conditions and circumstances of life are the opportunities that are given to us for working out the purpose of our existence. To use the opportunities properly, however, depends on us. The key to using the opportunities is to give what we have to those who need it. Lucky are those whose circumstances include a position of power. The experience is pleasant, almost intoxicating. And, what they can give is immense, and to so many. The better the opportunity, the greater the waste if it is not used. Whether our actions will change the world is secondary. Changing the world is ultimately the responsibility of the Divine, who knows all, can do all and will do all in Its time and Its way.

∞

First posted as a blog on 11 August 2017
Link: https://www.speakingtree.in/blog/pleased-to-ask-you-to-do-as-i-say

PUNCTUALITY

What Is Spiritual about Being Punctual?

Punctuality is the politeness of kings.

—Louis XVIII of France

As a society, we Indians are not exactly known for our punctuality. Using the cell phone to say, 'I am sorry I will be late because I am caught in a traffic jam', does not really help those affected by our being late. It might have been better to anticipate the traffic jam and start early. But the question is whether not being punctual is just bad manners? Lack of punctuality implies taking the liberty of doing what is convenient to me, or what makes me look important, while completely disregarding my fellow beings. Let us take a few examples.

Suppose the majority of those who are supposed to come for a meeting, or intend coming for a lecture, are late. If the event starts on time, those who come late not only miss something, they also disturb those who came on time. If the event is delayed, it penalizes those who came on time. They waste time while waiting for the event to begin, and might waste time at the end of the event if it ends late.

At a lunch or dinner, the host is ready to receive the guests a little before time—at least it is expected so, although at weddings the host proper, including the bride and bridegroom, are also sometimes late by *hours*. If the guests keep coming till three-four hours after the time at which they had been invited, not only everybody who comes may not be able to meet the others, the poor host is stuck with the event for five-six hours, and may take another couple of hours to wind up. What it means is that even if the dinner invitation was for 7.00 p.m., he may not be able to sleep till well past midnight.

If a doctor or lawyer or 'the boss' keeps patients or clients or 'subordinates' waiting because that makes him look busy and, therefore, important, he indeed has a mistaken notion of what makes a person truly good, great or important.

In all the above examples, a person shows utter disregard for his fellow beings. In contrast, spirituality implies seeing the Divine in all our fellow beings. When it comes to our divine essence, the other person is not only my equal, the other person is also 'me'. Hence, disregarding others and getting perverse pleasure by humiliating them is not only impolite; it is also unspiritual.

∞

First posted as a blog on 30 May 2014
Link: https://www.speakingtree.in/blog/what-is-spiritual-about-being-punctual

QUEUE

Queue: More Than a Line

An Englishman, even if he is alone, forms an orderly queue of one.

—George Mikes

A queue is more than a line in which people stand one behind the other waiting for their turn. It is also more than a symbol of order and discipline. It signifies respect for the rights of others. If somebody came before me, he has a right to be served before me, and I respect his right by standing in the queue behind him. A queue also signifies equality. The priority in a queue is determined by the order of arrival, or some other neutral criterion such as the alphabetical order. Priority cannot be claimed on the basis of caste, colour, creed, wealth, wisdom or gender. The 'queuing' habit is also a good indicator of the spiritual development of a person. Spirituality acknowledges the universal presence of the spirit of the Divine. The spirit binds all of us, and equalizes all of us. *Aham Brahmasmi* (I am Brahman) and *Tat Tvam*

Asi (you are That) are two of the most frequently quoted sentences from the Upanishads, acknowledging that while my fundamental reality is the Divine (Brahman), your fundamental reality is also the same. If I wish someone with folded hands and say 'namaste' or 'namaskar', what I am telling him is that I bow to the Divinity in him. In short, the idea of a queue is based on equality; and spirituality also acknowledges the equality of all creation. However, it is a paradox that this fundamental equality is forgotten in abodes of the Divine. In temples, the queue for 'darshan' may be jumped by jostling, by flaunting one's position or by making a hefty donation.

The queue serves an important function in banks, post offices, hospitals and bus stops by maintaining order and decency, and ensuring that the weak and the meek also get their turn. The tendency to be in a queue has important implications for driving. If I am behind someone, I should be content to stay behind unless there is a strong reason for overtaking and it is safe to overtake.

There are, of course, situations in which the principle of being in the queue needs to be willfully violated. For example, when it comes to promotions in jobs, performance should be encouraged by making merit rather than seniority the primary criterion. While boarding a bus, it makes sense to let the old and infirm jump the queue. Also, it is no sin to avoid being in a long queue by being an early bird or by avoiding peak hours or peak days. If being in a queue is inevitable, one may make use of the waiting time by reading (or these days, by playing with a rectangular pocket device, which is more than a phone) or by getting into a friendly non-intrusive but potentially productive chat with the person ahead of me or behind me. In short, there is no bar on using one's head to avoid or bypass queues in ways that do not trample on the rights of others. On the whole, however, the queue-forming habit is possibly a good and simple indicator of what is currently termed the 'spirituality quotient' of a person. In this respect, people fall into three broad categories: those who have a natural tendency to form a queue and stay in a queue, those who can be made to be in a queue and those who insist on jumping every queue.

(Related essay: 'Driving')

∞

First posted as a blog on 17 July 2015
Link: https://www.speakingtree.in/blog/queue-more-than-a-line

RELATIONSHIPS

Everybody Is a Relative

The inner loneliness can only be cured by the inner experience of union with the Divine; no human association can fill the void.

—Sri Aurobindo

We are all products of a relationship, the relationship that our mother had with our father. Their relationship by marriage led to our blood relationship with them. Relationships by blood or marriage are commonly considered the only real relationships. These relationships can be extended to second cousins and beyond, or restricted to parents, progeny and siblings. In practice, these relationships may be intimate, indifferent or incompatible, but they remain undeniable, and we may be forced to accept them on the basis of a DNA test if we try to deny them! Conventionally, in the Indian society, relationships based on blood or created by marriage have been considered sacrosanct and permanent, with well-defined duties, expectations and hierarchy, depending on the relationship. The reminders regarding the commitments based on these relationships keep returning with a vengeance in spite of the all-too-common family feuds and disputes. However, in today's world, in which materialism and utilitarianism are the new gods, the intimacy in these relationships is often guided by the suitability of the relative—suitability in terms of status and utility, which means what the relative can do for us.

In contrast with relationships by blood or marriage are friendships. Friendships are generally based on having a lot in common, such as age, opinions, language, hobbies, interests, level of education, socio-economic status, etc. Depending on some of these factors, we choose friends, and over time grow closer to them or start distancing ourselves from them. Distancing may be forced by geographical separation, preoccupation with the family or personal problems; or may be voluntary because the friends have taken to different paths and therefore do not have much in common any more. One of them might have sunk deeper in material comforts, and the other might have floated to the blissful world of spirituality. It is the freedom to deepen or dilute the relationship at will at any stage that makes many of us, especially young people, favour friendships over relationships based on blood or marriage. The enormous choice and flexibility makes compatibility the very basis of the friendships that survive the test of time. But true friendships are rare. Your true friend is always available, is willing to share with you even if he has very little, and is willing to suffer for your sake. It is difficult to have many such friends. Having even one such friend is indeed a luxury. Far more common are 'friendships' that flourish in the comfort zone but fade in a crisis.

There are many relationships that are a result of simply dealing with each other, such as business or professional relationships, the doctor-patient relationship, the teacher-student relationship, etc. Or, there are relationships based on sharing or having something in common. For example, neighbours sharing a neighbourhood; or colleagues working in the same organization also have a relationship. Or members of an association may all be in the same profession, might have gone to the same school or college, have the same disease, or have a passion for fighting for the same cause. These are functional relationships imposed by circumstances for a limited purpose. But one may discover some real friends through these relationships.

But the deepest and the most undeniable relationship is the spiritual relationship. Each of us is the embodiment of a soul, and all souls are individual condensations in an infinite pool of the universal spirit of the Creator. In simple words, all individuals are leaves of the same tree. In that sense, not only is everything relative, everybody is a relative. However, this fundamental uniting and equalizing relationship is too invisible to our ignorant mental consciousness. But within this basic relationship that we have with everybody and everything, animate and inanimate, there is a subset of relationships which Gary Zukav calls spiritual partnerships, that are based on a similar level of consciousness. They cannot be created by persuading others to become spiritual partners.

They cannot be created by asking others to change. The important thing to do is to change ourselves. As we grow and evolve spiritually, our relationship with our friends will change. With some of them, we will become closer. With some others, just the opposite will happen because the relationship will become less interesting. Further, we will attract new friends who will be at a similar stage of spiritual evolution. As Gary Zukav says, 'When a flower blooms, bees find it'. We will stumble upon new friends sometimes in totally unexpected ways. And, with these new friends, sometimes such an intimacy will develop in less than an hour that it would seem as if we have known each other for ages. In fact, perhaps we have. Gary Zukav compares individuals with actors who travel as part of the same troupe. They have played, by now, several roles in relation to one another as father, mother, child, sister, brother, friend, enemy, ruler, ruled, oppressor, oppressed, etc. Now they have an intimate relationship simply because they are members of the same troupe. Their current intimacy is completely independent of the role they are currently playing. Similarly, the people whom we become close to very easily and quickly are the ones with whom we have been related in many different ways in our previous lives (on earth and perhaps also elsewhere), and in the current life, we meet apparently accidentally and happen to be at a similar level of consciousness. That is how people on the spiritual path end up having, through many such discoveries, a spiritual family, which is quite apart from their biological family. It is within the spiritual family that there is scope for spiritual partnerships.

Spiritual partnerships are quite independent of age and gender. A person who is my grandmother today might have been my granddaughter in a previous life. Thus, her chronological age today might be 80 and mine only 20, but how does it matter if her 'true' age is 1000 lives plus 80, and mine 1,200 lives plus 20. Looked at in this way, the difference of 60 years in this life becomes meaningless. Further, in this life we may have no biological relationship at all and may just stumble upon each other. But the older relationships, because of being part of 'the same drama company', are enough to create remarkable spiritual affinity that leads to a spiritual partnership at amazing speed. How should the relationship between spiritual partners be? It should be, according to Sri Aurobindo, subordinated to the relationship with the Divine, and should be free from 'sexual impurity, jealousy, anger and egoistic demand'.

How does spiritual partnership differ from friendship? Even under the best of circumstances, what I can expect from a friend is that when I am in trouble, my friend will understand my difficulty, feel my sorrow, will try to do something concrete to help me and will try to provide me the best guidance that he is capable of. A spiritual partner will also do all these things, but in addition will also act as the trigger that ensures that I see in the present difficulty an opportunity for spiritual growth. As Gary Zukav says, 'Friends bond to ease the journey. Spiritual partners bond to grow spiritually... Spiritual partners travel beyond the boundaries of their comfort zones.'[1] Spiritual partners are not afraid of saying something that is right and will help the partner grow spiritually. At the same time, spiritual partners do not say something just to please the partner if it is not true, and will not help the partner grow spiritually. For example, if my spiritual partner is not getting along well with his wife, I will not unthinkingly join him in justifying his behaviour and condemning his wife. Even at the risk of annoying him, I will be neutral, show him his wife's point of view and will encourage him to grow spiritually by treating his wife as a manifestation of the Divine in spite of everything. I would show him that although he need not like his wife, he can still love her, and would explain to him how his *loving* her is in the interest of his own *peace of mind* and *spiritual growth* because the three invariably go together. Thus, as spiritual partners, we will make sure that our partners make the best use of all the opportunities that they get for spiritual growth, which is the very purpose of life. Hence, these partnerships make each individual grow spiritually more than he would if left entirely to himself. In short, spiritual partnerships are mutually uplifting relationships.

What is the fate of friendships and biological relationships when a person starts walking seriously on the spiritual path? Some of the older friendships may survive and move towards spiritual partnerships, many

---

[1]Winfrey, Oprah, 'Oprah Introduces the Concept That Changed How She Thinks about Relationships', Oprah Daily, 13 February 2022, https://bit.ly/3RIcjAa. Accessed on 19 July 2022.

of the older friendships fade away and new spiritual partnerships develop, creating for this person a spiritual family. But, what about the biological family? It is these relationships that pose a fundamental conflict to the spiritual seeker. While his path demands love without attachment, in his biological relationships he finds plenty of attachment without an avenue for expressing love.* Therefore, biological relationships, sooner or later, become an obstacle on the spiritual path. One solution to this dilemma has been a clean surgical cut. The spiritual seeker declares his intention to deviate from the conventional path, moves out of the house and requests that he be considered dead to his old self because now he has a new life. But Sri Aurobindo and The Mother's spiritual path is a highly life-affirming path which emphasizes an inner change without insisting on an outer change. Every difficulty is treated as an opportunity for inner work, not as a call to escape from life. This approach is not easy for the seeker to follow, and very difficult for his biological relatives to understand or accept. That is what makes Integral Yoga a razor's edge. The Mother advises us that all relationships should be replaced by 'a whole-hearted, unchanging, constant and egoless kindness and goodwill' and that all attachment should be rejected. But the difficulty arises from the biological family seeing lack of attachment (read indifference) written clearly on the seeker's face and resent it, but they do not see the 'kindness and goodwill' and therefore do not appreciate it. However, what is enough for the seeker is to know within how sincere his love still is for the family, although he cannot easily find a suitable avenue for expressing it. Further, the absence of understanding, or even presence of resentment within his family, should not prevent him from continuing his own spiritual journey. As Sri Aurobindo says, 'Relations after taking up yoga should be less based on a physical origin or the habits of the physical consciousness and more and more on the basis of sadhana—of sadhak with sadhaks, of others as souls travelling the same path or children of The Mother than in the ordinary way or with the old viewpoint.' Moreover, all biological families are not alike. In some cases, there may be scope for spiritual partnerships within the biological family. In some other cases, the biological family may be transformed by its uplifting contact with the spiritual seeker. In still other cases, there may be a gradual disruption in family ties. In Sri Aurobindo and The Mother's yoga, there can be, in general, no single rule applicable to all. In the context of family ties, a change in orientation will be inevitable; a transformed relationship where feasible and a severance where necessary.

We are living in a world that is fast evolving to assume a character that will be radically different from the one to which mankind has got accustomed over thousands of years. In this new world, spiritual relationship will replace family and friendship as the basis of loving interactions. At present, we can only imagine what the new world will be like. But this is one situation where reality might outstrip imagination. We are truly in for a future shock.

∞

*The person on the spiritual path should have universal love, and therefore his love for the biological family cannot disappear. As very simply put by Bernie Siegel, it is not necessary to like everybody, but it is possible to love everybody. But expression of love needs giving what one has to those who need it. Because of different interests and goals, the expression may become difficult. For example, the biological family might express its love for this person by giving him a new dress which he does not need. On the other hand, he might express his love for the biological family by trying to show them how they can grow spiritually through a difficulty that the family is going through—this is something they do not need; what they need is money, psychiatric consultation or legal advice. The result is that love may be there, but there is no avenue for expressing it. But the undeniable biological relationship leads to an attachment due to conditioning created by a long-standing relationship and the conventionally expected behaviour.

SEX WORK

Two Primitive Perennial Pursuits

The person who is sinless should be the first to throw a stone at her.

—The New Testament, John 8:7

Sex work is said to be the oldest profession in the world, and an aspiration to discover the deeper truths of existence—the oldest preoccupation of the awakened minds. The two pursuits seem to be poles apart; one seeks fleeting pleasure in hell, the other finds lasting happiness in heaven. But going by the principle that truth is never black and white, let us examine the issue dispassionately.

All trade involves giving what the trader has to the customer who needs it, and in turn the customer gives the trader some money. Giving what one has to someone who needs it without expecting anything in return is love; giving what one has and expecting something in return is trade. Trade is far more common than love. Even noble professions are turning into businesses. Teachers today sell their knowledge; doctors sell their skills; godmen sell spirituality; even devotees sell their offerings to God and expect a profit. The sex worker sells her body. But she is not the only one who sells her body. Waitresses soon discover that the deeper their necks, the higher the tips. One might say that the sex worker sells her body, but claims to love the customer. Therefore, she is a hypocrite. In favour of hypocrisy, Nirad Chaudhury has said that hypocrisy is the tribute that evil pays to good. That argument may be debatable, but doesn't all selling involve hypocrisy? Traders claim to give discounts because they want us to save money, while they actually want us to spend money. All ads claim to sell products which will make us happier, healthier, richer or prettier; none of them admit that they want our money. In short, all trade is sugar-coated with love. But even fake love is better than greed, anger, jealousy and hatred.

There is, in Indian mythology, a sex worker named Pingala. She was once waiting eagerly for a customer, who she expected would pay her very well. When the customer finally did not come, she was frustrated. The frustration led her to an insight: 'Instead of waiting so impatiently for someone who will come and go, why not get attached to the One who will be always with me and give me eternal joy?' Thus, the disappointment transformed her from a sex worker into a devotee of the Divine. The story has at least two lessons. First, that difficulties and unpleasant experiences are opportunities for spiritual growth. And second, that nobody is beyond redemption. A sex worker is also God's child, and He accepts her when she turns to Him.

A sex worker can not only let herself be transformed, she can also teach. Among the 24 gurus of Dattatreya, one was a sex worker. He said that a sex worker gives and receives artificial love. Neither the artificial love gives her any happiness, nor is she satisfied with the payment. On reflection, he had realized that we are all like sex workers, and the world is full of our customers. We look for happiness in our customers, the customers enjoy exploiting us, the returns are inadequate and we remain perpetually dissatisfied. Therefore, Dattatreya decided that he would not depend on the world for happiness, but would seek, like Pingala, the source of eternal joy within. In fact, one of the major outcomes of walking the spiritual path is exactly this. Our happiness becomes independent of external circumstances. Freedom from dependence on external circumstances is liberation, or moksha. Thus, one does not have to die to experience moksha; it is available in this world, in this life. And, Dattatreya was led to moksha by reflecting over the life of a sex worker.

Saying that a sex worker can be transformed and can inspire others to transform are by no means arguments in support of sex work. All that these arguments imply is the possibility of the best residing in the worst of situations. Sex work is the oldest profession, and has survived all social reforms. The reason behind its persistence is the persistence of supply and demand. Social injustice forces some women to sell the body at the expense of the soul to, paradoxically, keep the body and soul together. That ensures the supply. The demand is ensured by some men who are so engrossed in lust that they become blind to all the better pleasures of the world. The blindness that finds solace only in dark pleasures reflects a low level of consciousness. Hence, like all the other problems of human existence, this problem will also be wiped out only by a rise in the level of consciousness of the human race.

SHOPPING

Exchange of Money and Material

For some, shopping is an art; for others, it's a sport. It can be a vice and it can be a cause. Some love it. Some hate it. Rarely is someone indifferent.

—Pamela Klaffke

For the rich, shopping is a pastime; for the not so rich, it is a necessity; and for the depressed, it can be therapy. But for everyone, shopping is also an interaction and an exchange—both are opportunities for spiritual growth, which is the highest purpose of human life.

Interaction

Spiritually, every interaction should begin with the recognition of the Divine, inherent in the other person, so that this awareness continues throughout the interaction and influences its quality. If this seems unrealistic, what then is the 'namaste' with which the interaction begins? 'Namaste' means bowing to the divinity of the person in front of us; the fact that two pairs of hands participate in the 'namaste' with its meaning seldom passing through their heads is something different. The implication of the meaning behind the ritual is that it places the shopkeeper and the customer on an equal footing. Since both are manifestations of the same Divine, at a deeper level they are both equal. But on the surface, they are unequal, at least temporarily. Although the customer has the money that the shopkeeper needs, and the shopkeeper has the goods that the customer wants, customer is considered king because he has the liberty to buy the goods from anywhere, whereas each shopkeeper needs to succeed in selling to at least somebody to make a living. The customer sometimes does behave like the king (or queen). For example, a shopkeeper might bring a hundred saris down from the shelves and spread them out to make them look more attractive. And, finally, the lady may just get up and leave the shop because she did not like any of them: a good opportunity for the shopkeeper to practise equanimity (*samattva*). But the customer has wasted the opportunity of being in a position to think of somebody else. Thinking of somebody else with compassion is the path to spiritual progress. If she had thought of the shopkeeper with compassion, she would have given him a better idea of the type of sari she is looking for and discouraged him from bringing the saris down and spreading them out by pointing out a few that she would like to have a better look at. 'Thinking of somebody else' applies also to the shopkeeper. If he tries to guide the customer properly towards what will meet the needs of the customer instead of trying to foist on the customer the costliest stuff that he has in stock, he will be using the opportunity properly to fulfil the purpose of his life. Instead, sometimes he can sense that a woman has developed a fancy for a particular sari and he knows that she also knows that she won't get exactly the same sari elsewhere. He then tries to exploit her weakness to extract the highest possible price, and may even repent why he did not quote a still higher price to start with.

Exchange

Shopping, besides being an interaction, is also an exchange. In the process of shopping, money and material change hands. The material is a fixed entity, but the amount of money that may pass from the customer to the shopkeeper is negotiable. That is what leads to bargaining. Bargaining is a tug of war between the customer and the shopkeeper on behalf of their pockets; it is essentially 'my pocket' versus 'your pocket'. If you and me are the same, as is spiritually true, what difference does it make if a few rupees stay in your pocket or mine? But sometimes, it is heart-wrenching to see the customer's miserliness and tenacity pitted against the shopkeeper's desperation and dependence. I have seen educated well-to-do women use power and persuasion to force a petty peddler operating from a pavement part with a piece of art for a pittance, exploiting the poor man's need for a few pennies. She finally gets it at a price that leaves hardly any profit for the peddler, although she knows that the object is worth a lot more and she can afford to pay what it is worth. Then she may come and display it in the living room, and at the slightest provocation, boast that she bought it at an emporium for an amount which is 10 times the amount that she had actually paid.

Just contrast the following three scenarios, although in each the end result is that a deal has been concluded: the customer has bought and the trader has sold something, and they are both reflecting over the interaction.

Scenario One

Customer: I have been clever enough to get it dirt cheap.

Shopkeeper: A few more such customers, and I would starve. They can splurge on useless luxuries, but turn so mean while bargaining with a poor man.

Scenario Two

Customer: I did not really need the object. But I am happy I could support the shopkeeper. Hope enough reaches the artisan also, who spent days making it.

Shopkeeper: Good decent customer. What a contrast with those who waste so much time for a few pennies and leave me with a headache.

Scenario Three

Customer: I had the money, and he needed it. By accepting from me what I had, the shopkeeper helped me fulfil the purpose of my life.

Shopkeeper: The customer gave me so much joy. She not only helped me make a living, she made my day so much better.

Shopping is only an example of the several interactions we have in which the two interacting individuals are temporarily on an unequal footing. It could be the interaction with a taxi driver, with a porter at the railway station or with the boy who issues parking tickets. Let us remember that first, the inequality is temporary. Not only are we equal at a spiritual level, eventually life levels everybody also at the visible worldly level. Second, with a minor twist of destiny, we could have been in each other's place. Let us not get so carried away by short-lived superficial inequality that we lose the opportunity that the interaction provides for giving a little joy to somebody, inevitably getting back in the process immense joy ourselves, and also fulfilling the purpose of our own life.

∞

First posted as a blog on 8 August 2017
Link: https://www.speakingtree.in/blog/exchange-of-money-and-material

TOUCH

Being Touchy about Touch

One hug always equals two...
One for them and one for you.

—Aine Belton

In his book, *Intimate Behavior*, Desmond Morris says that our addiction to touch begins in the womb. In the womb, the foetus is constantly surrounded by the warm amniotic fluid, to which it gets so accustomed that when its skin is exposed to the cold air outside, it gets a rude shock, which we try to assuage by immediately wrapping it up in a cloth. An intimate warm touch as a symbol of love and security is something that stays with us throughout life. That is why many of us find it necessary to sleep with at least a bed sheet covering us even when it is not cold. The bed sheet may be necessary, but is seldom sufficient to meet our basic needs for giving and receiving love. And, touch is one of the most potent, although silent, universal languages of love. So deprived do people feel if there is nobody to touch them that in today's commerce-driven world, selling hugs is an acceptable and viable business. If you have any doubts, just Google 'hugs on sale': my search in December 2017 yielded 24,900,000 results in 0.38 seconds!

If touch is a symbol of love, let us first get this much-used, and abused, word 'love' out of the way. Love is the antidote to ego that has been planted in us so that we can fulfil the purpose of life. Fulfilment of the purpose of life depends on moving from the sense of division towards that of oneness. Ego divides, and it is love that unites. Giving as well as receiving love are both human needs, and both help us fulfil the purpose of life. We give love when breakdown of the ego barrier makes us feel one with the other person. This is easy to understand. What is a little more difficult to understand is that we willingly receive love also only from someone with whom we feel one. Suppose a child is angry with the parent. If the parent tries to make up by trying to hug the child, the first response of the child is to reject the hug. Partners do the same. When they quarrel, they say, 'I want nothing from you, not even a glass of water': here, asking for or accepting 'water' is a symbol of love. Assertion of total self-reliance is an expression of the ego. Willingness to accept love, therefore, needs transcending the ego. Since receiving love also depends on breakdown of the ego barrier, it abolishes division, leads to oneness and fulfils the purpose of life. Inviting somebody to dinner is an expression of love; accepting the invitation is also an expression of love.

If love is natural, necessary and enjoyable, why is it sometimes frowned upon? That is because there are many rungs of love. The first rung is to love somebody because it makes me happy. The second rung is to love somebody because it makes both of us happy. The third rung is to love because it makes the other person happy. Any love is better than no love at all, but the first rung can be dangerous. If loving somebody makes me happy, but the other person does not accept my love, there are two possibilities. The healthy option is to rise to the second rung, and decide not to shower my love on this person because my love is unable to make this person happy. The unhealthy option is to get angry with this person for not accepting my love. The anger can take dangerous turns, as in the case of some boys who throw acid on the face of a girl who has rejected their love. The basic principle to understand is that while love is a highly desirable emotion, it cannot be, and should not be, expressed where it is not needed. Love can be expressed only to someone who needs it, only to someone who is willing to accept it the way I want to express it. This becomes particularly important when love is expressed through touch.

Discussions about 'good touch' and 'bad touch' are primarily centred around two points: one, which part of the body can or cannot be touched; and two, who may or may not touch whom. These are criteria that would vary with culture, time and place. What is more important is what the consciousness is while touching and how it is affected by the touch. If the consciousness is high and is further uplifted by the touch, it is a good touch; if the consciousness is low and falls as a result of the touch, it is a bad touch. A simpler way to put it would be to say that if the aim of the touch is primarily to give joy to the person who is being touched, it is a good touch; if the primary aim is to get joy by touching irrespective of how the touched person feels, it is a bad touch. In short, if the joy flows from Me to You, it is a good touch; if the joy is snatched from You to Me, it is a bad touch. Which way the joy flows may not always be obvious to onlookers. The person who knows it best is the person who touches; next best it is known to the person who is being touched.

On who may or may not touch whom, the less said the better. In spite of the taboos and embarrassment that go with such disclosures, studies have repeatedly shown that the bad touch comes, in majority of cases, from someone who is within the family, is close to the family or is in a position in which he is least likely to be suspected of the offence. Therefore, to assume that if an uncle touches his niece, it is always a good touch is making a highly questionable assumption. This fact has at least two important corollaries. First, if the 'uncle' seems to be focused on the joy he is getting, have the courage to say 'no' to his hug. Secondly, do not say 'no' to a hug just because it is coming from someone who is biologically not related to you. The second corollary is likely to be more important in the world that is emerging. The world is moving towards a higher level of consciousness, a world in which biological relationships will matter less than spiritual relationships, which are based on a deeper affinity due to a similar level of consciousness. Sri Aurobindo and The Mother talked about this evolutionary movement about a hundred years ago; many more like Gary Zukav are talking about it today. The conventional society has no problem if a brother gives a hug to his sister, but is shocked if the hug comes from a friend. Times are coming when the objective criteria of intimacy based on biological relationship will have to give way to subjective criteria based on consciousness.

In December 2017, a schoolboy gave a hug to a girl in the school premises. Not only were both the students suspended, even the parents of the children concerned were pulled up for not having brought up their children well.[1] The parents influence their children more by example than by what they tell the children to do or not to do. If the parents of these children taught them to give and accept hugs by hugging the children and each other, it should be viewed as excellent upbringing. It is difficult to understand why, in our society, partners are shy of hugging each other when their children are around, while they have no hesitation in fighting with each other in front of their children. What sets a better example for the children—hugging or fighting—should not be a difficult question to answer.

What a wonderful arrangement the good Lord has made! Through love, which we all need and enjoy, we also fulfil the purpose of life. Shouldn't we be grateful to the Lord for it, and make good use of this tool in the natural course of life rather than depend upon someone to sell us a hug?

---

[1] Padanna, Ashraf, 'The Indian Teenagers Who Were Expelled from School for Hugging', BBC, 22 December 2017, https://bbc.in/3Plv6zJ. Accessed on 19 July 2022.

WAR

Made in Minds, Fought in Fields

Those that can control their senses can acquire the sovereignty of the whole world.

(Vidura to Yudhishthira in the Mahabharata)

A highly revered scripture, the Gita, is a lesson delivered in the battlefield by the divine teacher, Sri Krishna, to a human disciple, Arjuna. And, interestingly, the disciple did not want to fight, but it is the teacher who told him that his reluctance to fight would mean that he is shirking from his dharma, his duty. By the end of the Gita, Krishna brings Arjuna to a point where he is ready and willing to fight. It is often asked how Krishna, an incarnation of God, could support the violence that war inevitably involves. To justify it, sometimes it is said that the war of Mahabharata, which Krishna supported, is only symbolic of the war within: the conflict that we have between our lower nature and our higher nature. While the war within is a reality of spiritual life, using it as a justification for the war of Mahabharata is not necessary.

The war on the physical plane can also be spiritual, and can be fought in a spiritual manner. To understand this, there are three questions about the war of Mahabharata which one needs to consider: why, when and how.

Why? The war of Mahabharata was fought not for personal glory or benefit but *to defend justice from injustice*. Good and evil are the dualities that are a part of the human world at its present level of consciousness. And, there are some individuals who are temperamentally suited to fight evil. These individuals, whose personality has dominant rajas and substantial sattva but negligible tamas were called Kshatriyas, and it was considered their duty to protect the society from evil. Arjuna was a model Kshatriya and, therefore, when he recoiled from war, he was reminded what his duty was.

When? The war of Mahabharata was fought *when all peaceful options had been exhausted*. Sri Krishna had gone to the Kauravas as an emissary of the Pandavas to make Duryodhana see reason. He also suggested a compromise: if Duryodhana kept the vast empire but parted with just five villages, even that would satisfy the Pandavas. But Duryodhana retorted by saying that he would not part with even the land occupied by the tip of a needle.

The 'why' and 'when' of a war tell us whether the war is justified or unjustified, righteous or unrighteous. There have been young men who have refused to fight in a war when they felt that the war to which their country was sending them was an unjustified one. These people are called conscientious objectors, and their right to refuse has been upheld by the United Nations since 1995.

How? The war of Mahabharata was fought *openly*, not by guerrilla warfare or terrorism. It involved only the armies; the *civilians were not involved*. Even the war had its norms, which were, by and large, respected. Finally, and most importantly, Arjuna was told to fight without hatred for the Kauravas. He was told to fight as an instrument of the Divine, because the decision that the Kauravas must die had already been taken by the Divine. Arjuna was thus merely fulfilling the Divine Will.

Killing without hatred may seem like an impossibility, but it can be done because the psychic being (the dynamic aspect of the soul) can be contacted and brought forward even in war. In fact, a war is an opportunity to test how far one can contact the Divine within, and see the Divine also in the enemy, even when involved in intense activity, surrounded by violence, and when the mind is dominated by divisive patriotic feelings. Not having hatred for the enemy is also rational. The soldiers facing each other have no personal enmity. They are both merely doing their duties. There are several stories of compassion towards the enemy in wars. Pilots have escorted enemy planes to safety when the enemy plane had severely injured soldiers. The navy has sunk an enemy ship and then rescued the passengers, and soldiers have offered water to thirsty enemy soldiers.[1] Compassion towards someone who could have killed you is hard, and that is why it is all the more spiritually significant. War is to some an opportunity to

---

[1] V., Marc, 'Ten Extraordinary Acts of Compassion in Wartime', *Listverse*, 19 December 2013, https://bit.ly/3uXzdJY. Accessed on 19 July 2022.

act from the highest level of consciousness and thereby manifest the divinity within.

(Related essay: 'Army')

www.ingramcontent.com/pod-product-compliance
Lightning Source LLC
Chambersburg PA
CBHW042142160426
43201CB00022B/2371